MANUFACTURING

THIRD EDITION

Ferguson
An imprint of Infobase Publishing

Careers in Focus: Manufacturing, Third Edition

Copyright © 2008 by Infobase Publishing

All rights reserved. No part of this book may be reproduced or utilized in any form or by any means, electronic or mechanical, including photocopying, recording, or by any information storage or retrieval systems, without permission in writing from the publisher. For information contact

Ferguson
An imprint of Infobase Publishing
132 West 31st Street
New York NY 10001

Library of Congress Cataloging-in-Publication Data

Careers in focus : manufacturing. — 3rd ed.
    p. cm.
  Includes index.
  ISBN-13: 978-0-8160-7273-6
  ISBN-10: 0-8160-7273-6
  1. Industrial technicians—Vocational guidance. 2. Industrial engineering—Vocational guidance. I. J.G. Ferguson Publishing Company. II. Title: Manufacturing.
  TA158.C36 2008
  670.23—dc22
                                        2007037485

Ferguson books are available at special discounts when purchased in bulk quantities for businesses, associations, institutions, or sales promotions. Please call our Special Sales Department in New York at (212) 967-8800 or (800) 322-8755.

You can find Ferguson on the World Wide Web at http://www.fergpubco.com

Text design by David Strelecky
Cover design by Salvatore Luongo

Printed in the United States of America

MP MSRF 10 9 8 7 6 5 4 3 2 1

This book is printed on acid-free paper.

Table of Contents

Introduction

Manufacturing covers a wide range of industries, including food, beverage, pharmaceuticals, iron and steel, textiles, lumber, tobacco, automobiles, aerospace, and petrochemicals. In manufacturing, there are two types of goods produced: durable and nondurable. Durable goods have a long life span and hold up over time; examples of durable goods are cars, airplanes, and washing machines. Nondurable goods have a shorter life span and include such products as food, cosmetics, and clothing.

One of the most promising segments of the manufacturing workforce is engineering. Engineers' work focuses on research, development, analysis, planning, survey, application, facility evaluation, and more. They may manage a staff or manage projects from start to finish. Those responsible for research and development refine the production process and make recommendations to their companies based on their research findings. Engineers work with computers, in robotics development and implementation, and plant safety. Technicians, who work closely with and assist engineers in manufacturing, help to execute various projects by conducting research, running tests, and fulfilling other duties.

Today, there are a declining number of manufacturing jobs, and the jobs that exist are less viable than they were 10 or 20 years ago. One reason for the decline in domestic manufacturing is that many factories continue to relocate to foreign countries with lower labor and material costs. As a result, labor unions have lost some of their strength to negotiate for better contracts and wages for manufacturing workers. The other key reason for the continuing decrease in factory jobs is automation. To cut labor costs, manufacturers are replacing much of their labor force with robotics-based machinery. In many cases, these machines are more efficient and productive than human workers. In order to remain competitive, many companies are striving to become even more automated, which will in turn eliminate even more jobs. However, while many assembly line jobs will disappear, the demand for engineers—the individuals who program, install, and maintain the automated machinery—should be strong.

Textile and apparel manufacturing is projected to decline more than any other manufacturing industry through 2014, due primarily to increasing imports. However, pharmaceutical manufacturing is one industry segment that is expected to show healthy employment growth. A growing population, particularly among the elderly, and the frequent introduction of new drugs, medicinals, and botanicals to the public will continue to bolster the pharmaceutical market.

Each article in this book discusses in detail a particular occupation in the manufacturing field. The articles in *Careers in Focus: Manufacturing* appear in Ferguson's *Encyclopedia of Careers and Vocational Guidance,* but have been updated and revised with the latest information from the U.S. Department of Labor, professional organizations, and other sources. The following paragraphs detail the sections and features that appear in the book.

The **Quick Facts** section provides a brief summary of the career including recommended school subjects, personal skills, work environment, minimum educational requirements, salary ranges, certification or licensing requirements, and employment outlook. This section also provides acronyms and identification numbers for the following government classification indexes: the *Dictionary of Occupational Titles* (DOT), the *Guide for Occupational Exploration* (GOE), the National Occupational Classification (NOC) Index, and the Occupational Information Network (O*NET)-Standard Occupational Classification System (SOC) index. The DOT, GOE, and O*NET-SOC indexes have been created by the U.S. government; the NOC index is Canada's career-classification system. Readers can use the identification numbers listed in the Quick Facts section to access further information about a career. Print editions of the DOT (*Dictionary of Occupational Titles.* Indianapolis, Ind.: JIST Works, 1991) and GOE (*Guide for Occupational Exploration.* Indianapolis, Ind.: JIST Works, 2001) are available at libraries. Electronic versions of the NOC (http://www23.hrdc-drhc.gc.ca) and O*NET-SOC (http://online.onetcenter.org) are available on the Internet. When no DOT, GOE, NOC, or O*NET-SOC numbers are present, this means that the U.S. Department of Labor or Human Resources Development Canada have not created a numerical designation for this career. In this instance, you will see the acronym "N/A," or not available.

The **Overview** section is a brief introductory description of the duties and responsibilities involved in this career. Oftentimes, a career may have a variety of job titles. When this is the case, alternative career titles are presented. Employment statistics are also provided, when available. The **History** section describes the history of the particular job as it relates to the overall development of its industry or field. **The Job** describes the primary and secondary duties of the job. **Requirements** discusses high school and postsecondary education and training requirements, any certification or licensing that is necessary, and other personal requirements for success in the job. **Exploring** offers suggestions on how to gain experience in or knowledge of the particular job before making a firm educational and financial commitment. The focus is on what can be done while still in high school (or in the early years of college) to gain a better understanding of the job. The **Employers** section gives an overview of typical places of employment for the job. **Starting Out** discusses the best ways to land that first job, be it through the college career services office, newspaper ads, Internet employment sites, or personal contact. The **Advancement** section describes what kind of career path to expect from the job and how to get there. **Earnings** lists salary ranges and describes the typical fringe benefits. The **Work Environment** section describes the typical surroundings and conditions of employment—whether indoors or outdoors, noisy or quiet, social or independent. Also discussed are typical hours worked, any seasonal fluctuations, and the stresses and strains of the job. The **Outlook** section summarizes the job in terms of the general economy and industry projections. For the most part, Outlook information is obtained from the U.S. Bureau of Labor Statistics and is supplemented by information gathered from professional associations. Job growth terms follow those used in the *Occupational Outlook Handbook*. Growth described as "much faster than the average" means an increase of 27 percent or more. Growth described as "faster than the average" means an increase of 18 to 26 percent. Growth described as "about as fast as the average" means an increase of 9 to 17 percent. Growth described as "more slowly than the average" means an increase of 0 to 8 percent. "Decline" means a decrease by any amount. Each article ends with **For More Information,** which lists organizations that provide information on training, education, internships, scholarships, and job placement.

Careers in Focus: Manufacturing also includes photographs, informative sidebars, and interviews with professionals in the field.

Aerospace Engineers

OVERVIEW

Aerospace engineering encompasses the fields of aeronautical (aircraft) and astronautical (spacecraft) engineering. *Aerospace engineers* work in teams to design, build, and test machines that fly within the earth's atmosphere and beyond. Although aerospace science is a very specialized discipline, it is also considered one of the most diverse. This field of engineering draws from such subjects as physics, mathematics, earth science, aerodynamics, and biology. Some aerospace engineers specialize in designing one complete machine, perhaps a commercial aircraft, whereas others focus on separate components such as for missile guidance systems. There are approximately 76,000 aerospace engineers working in the United States.

HISTORY

The roots of aerospace engineering can be traced as far back as when people first dreamed of being able to fly. Thousands of years ago, the Chinese developed kites and later experimented with gunpowder as a source of propulsion. In the 15th century, artist Leonardo da Vinci created drawings of two devices that were designed to fly. One, the ornithopter, was supposed to fly the way birds do, by flapping its wings; the other was designed as a rotating screw, closer in form to today's helicopter.

In 1783, Joseph and Jacques Montgolfier of France designed the first hot-air balloon that could be used for manned flight. In 1799, an English baron, Sir George Cayley, designed an aircraft that was one of the first not to be considered "lighter than air," as balloons were. He developed a fixed-wing structure that led to his creation of the first

QUICK FACTS

School Subjects
Mathematics
Physics

Personal Skills
Mechanical/manipulative
Technical/scientific

Work Environment
Primarily indoors
Primarily one location

Minimum Education Level
Bachelor's degree

Salary Range
$50,993 to $87,610 to
  $124,550+

Certification or Licensing
Required by certain states

Outlook
More slowly than the average

DOT
002

GOE
02.07.04

NOC
2146

O*NET-SOC
17-2011.00

glider in 1849. Much experimentation was performed in gliders and the science of aerodynamics through the late 1800s. In 1903, the first mechanically powered and controlled flight was completed in a craft designed by Orville and Wilbur Wright. The big boost in airplane development occurred during World War I. In the early years of the war, aeronautical engineering encompassed a variety of engineering skills applied toward the development of flying machines. Civil engineering principles were used in structural design, while early airplane engines were devised by automobile engineers. Aerodynamic design itself was primarily empirical, with many answers coming from liquid flow concepts established in marine engineering.

The evolution of the airplane continued during both world wars, with steady technological developments in materials science, propulsion, avionics, and stability and control. Airplanes became larger and faster. Airplanes are commonplace today, but commercial flight became a frequent mode of transportation only as recently as the 1960s and 1970s.

Robert Goddard developed and flew the first liquid-propelled rocket in 1926. The technology behind liquid propulsion continued to evolve, and the first U.S. liquid rocket engine was tested in 1938. More sophisticated rockets were eventually created to enable aircraft to be launched into space. The world's first artificial satellite, *Sputnik I*, was launched by the Soviets in 1957. In 1961, President John F. Kennedy urged the United States to be the first country to put a

Aerospace engineers study documents at a Beechcraft aircraft factory. *(David R. Frazier, The Image Works)*

man on the moon; on July 20, 1969, astronauts Neil Armstrong and Edwin Aldrin Jr. accomplished that goal.

Today, aerospace engineers design spacecraft that explore beyond the earth's atmosphere. They create missiles and military aircraft of many types, such as fighters, bombers, observers, and transports. Today's engineers go beyond the dreams of merely learning to fly. For example, in 1998, the United States and 15 other countries began a series of joint missions into space to assemble a planned International Space Station. On the ground, space professionals, including aerospace engineers, have played a vital role in developing equipment that is used on the station.

THE JOB

Although the creation of aircraft and spacecraft involve professionals from many branches of engineering (e.g., materials, electrical, and mechanical), aerospace engineers in particular are responsible for the total design of the craft, including its shape, performance, propulsion, and guidance control system. In the field of aerospace engineering, professional responsibilities vary widely depending on the specific job description. *Aeronautical engineers* work specifically with aircraft systems, and *astronautical engineers* specialize in spacecraft systems.

Throughout their education and training, aerospace engineers thoroughly learn the complexities involved in how materials and structures perform under tremendous stress. In general, they are called upon to apply their knowledge of the following subjects: propulsion, aerodynamics, thermodynamics, fluid mechanics, flight mechanics, and structural analysis. Less technically scientific issues must also often be dealt with, such as cost analysis, reliability studies, maintainability, operations research, marketing, and management.

There are many professional titles given to certain aerospace engineers. *Analytical engineers* use engineering and mathematical theory to solve questions that arise during the design phase. *Stress analysts* determine how the weight and loads of structures behave under a variety of conditions. This analysis is performed with computers and complex formulas.

Computational fluid dynamic (CFD) engineers use sophisticated high-speed computers to develop models used in the study of fluid dynamics. Using simulated systems, they determine how elements flow around objects; simulation saves time and money and eliminates risks involved with actual testing. As computers become more complex, so do the tasks of the CFD engineer.

Design aerospace engineers draw from the expertise of many other specialists. They devise the overall structure of components and entire crafts, meeting the specifications developed by those more specialized in aerodynamics, astrodynamics, and structural engineering. Design engineers use computer-aided design programs for many of their tasks. *Manufacturing aerospace engineers* develop the plans for producing the complex components that make up aircraft and spacecraft. They work with the designers to ensure that the plans are economically feasible and will produce efficient, effective components.

Materials aerospace engineers determine the suitability of the various materials that are used to produce aerospace vehicles. Aircraft and spacecraft require the appropriate tensile strength, density, and rigidity for the particular environments they are subjected to. Determining how materials such as steel, glass, and even chemical compounds react to temperature and stress is an important part of the materials engineer's responsibilities.

Quality control is a task that aerospace engineers perform throughout the development, design, and manufacturing processes. The finished product must be evaluated for its reliability, vulnerability, and how it is to be maintained and supported.

Marketing and sales aerospace engineers work with customers, usually industrial corporations and the government, informing them of product performance. They act as a liaison between the technical engineers and the clients to help ensure that the products delivered are performing as planned. Sales engineers also need to anticipate the needs of the customer, as far ahead as possible, to inform their companies of potential marketing opportunities. They also keep abreast of their competitors and need to understand how to structure contracts effectively.

REQUIREMENTS

High School
While in high school, follow a college preparatory program. Doing well in mathematics and science classes is vital if you want to pursue a career in any type of engineering field. The American Society for Engineering Education advises students to take calculus and trigonometry in high school, as well as laboratory science classes. Such courses provide the skills you'll need for problem solving, an essential skill in any type of engineering.

Postsecondary Training
Aerospace engineers need a bachelor's degree to enter the field. More advanced degrees are necessary for those interested in teaching or research and development positions.

While a major in aerospace engineering is the norm, other majors are acceptable. For example, the National Aeronautics and Space Administration (NASA) recommends a degree in any of a variety of disciplines, including biomedical engineering, ceramics engineering, chemistry, industrial engineering, materials science, metallurgy, optical engineering, and oceanography. You should make sure the college you choose has an accredited engineering program. The Accreditation Board for Engineering and Technology (ABET) sets minimum education standards for programs in these fields. Graduation from an ABET-accredited school is a requirement for becoming licensed in many states, so it is important to select an accredited school. Currently, approximately 360 colleges and universities offer ABET-accredited engineering programs. Visit ABET's Web site (http://www.abet.org) for a listing of accredited schools.

Some aerospace engineers complete master's degrees and even doctoral work before entering this field. Advanced degrees can significantly increase an engineer's earnings. Students continuing on to graduate school will study research and development, with a thesis required for a master's degree and a dissertation for a doctorate. About one-third of all aerospace engineers go on to graduate school to get a master's degree.

Certification or Licensing

Most states require engineers to be licensed. There are two levels of licensing for engineers. Professional engineers (PEs) have graduated from an accredited engineering curriculum, have four years of engineering experience, and have passed a written exam. Engineering graduates need not wait until they have four years experience, however, to start the licensure process. Those who pass the Fundamentals of Engineering examination after graduating are called engineers in training (EITs) or engineer interns. The EIT certification usually is valid for 10 years. After acquiring suitable work experience, EITs can take the second examination, the Principles and Practice of Engineering exam, to gain full PE licensure.

In order to ensure that aerospace engineers are kept up-to-date on their quickly changing field, many states have imposed continuing education requirements for relicensure.

Other Requirements

Aerospace engineers should enjoy completing detailed work, problem solving, and participating in group efforts. Mathematical, science, and computer skills are a must. Equally important, however, are the abilities to communicate ideas, share in teamwork, and visualize the forms and functions of structures. Curiosity, inventiveness, and the willingness to continue to learn from experiences are excellent qualities to have for this type of work.

EXPLORING

If you like to work on model airplanes and rockets, you may be a good candidate for an aerospace engineering career. Consider working on special research assignments supervised by your science and math teachers. You may also want to try working on cars and boats, which provides a good opportunity to discover more about aerodynamics. A part-time job with a local manufacturer can give you some exposure to product engineering and development.

Exciting opportunities are often available at summer camps and academic programs throughout the country. For instance, the University of North Dakota presents an aerospace camp focusing on study and career exploration that includes instruction in model rocketry and flight. However, admission to the camp is competitive; the camp usually consists of two eight-day programs for 32 students each. (See the end of this article for more information.)

It is also a good idea to join a science club while in high school. For example, the Junior Engineering Technical Society provides members with opportunities to enter academic competitions, explore career opportunities, and design model structures. Contact information is available at the end of this article.

Aerospace America (http://www.aiaa.org/aerospace), published by the American Institute of Aeronautics and Astronautics, is a helpful magazine for exploring careers in aerospace.

EMPLOYERS

The U.S. Department of Labor reports that approximately 76,000 aerospace engineers are employed in the United States. Many aircraft-related engineering jobs are found in Alabama, California, and Florida, where large aerospace companies are located. Approximately 60 percent of all aerospace engineers work in products and parts manufacturing. Government agencies such as the U.S. Department of Defense and NASA employ approximately 12 percent of aerospace engineers. Other employers include engineering services, research and testing services, and electronics manufacturers.

STARTING OUT

Many students begin their careers while completing their studies through work-study arrangements that sometimes turn into full-time jobs. Most aerospace manufacturers actively recruit engineering students, conducting on-campus interviews and other activities to locate the best candidates. Students preparing to graduate can also send out resumes to companies active in the aerospace industry and arrange interviews. Many colleges and universities also staff career services offices, which are often good places to find leads for new job openings.

Students can also apply directly to agencies of the federal government concerned with aerospace development and implementation. Applications can be made through the Office of Personnel Management or through an agency's own hiring department.

Professional associations, such as the National Society of Professional Engineers and the American Institute of Aeronautics and Astronautics, offer job placement services, including career advice, job listings, and training. Their Web addresses are listed at the end of this article.

ADVANCEMENT

As in most engineering fields, there tends to be a hierarchy of workers in the various divisions of aerospace engineering. This is true in research, design and development, production, and teaching. In an entry-level job, one is considered simply an engineer, perhaps a junior engineer. After a certain amount of experience is gained, depending on the position, one moves on to work as a *project engineer*, supervising others. Then, as a *managing engineer*, one has further responsibilities over a number of project engineers and their teams. At the top of the hierarchy is the position of *chief engineer*, which involves authority over managing engineers and additional decision-making responsibilities.

As engineers move up the career ladder, the type of responsibilities they have tend to change. Junior engineers are highly involved in technical matters and scientific problem solving. As managers and chiefs, engineers have the responsibilities of supervising, cost analyzing, and relating with clients.

All engineers must continue to learn and study technological progress throughout their careers. It is important to keep abreast of engineering advancements and trends by reading industry journals and taking courses. Such courses are offered by professional associations or colleges. In aerospace engineering especially, changes occur rapidly, and those who seek promotions must be prepared. Those who are employed by colleges and universities must continue teaching and conducting research if they want to have tenured (more guaranteed) faculty positions.

EARNINGS

In 2006, the median salary for all aerospace engineers was about $87,610 per year, according to the U.S. Department of Labor. Experienced engineers employed by the federal government tended to earn more, with a mean salary of $97,240. Federal employees, however, enjoy greater job security and often more generous vacation and retirement benefits. The most experienced aerospace engineers earned salaries of more than $124,550 annually.

Aerospace engineers with bachelor's degrees earn average starting salaries of $50,993 per year, according to a 2005 salary survey conducted by the National Association of Colleges and Employers. With a master's degree, candidates were offered $62,930, and with a Ph.D., $72,529.

All engineers can expect to receive vacation and sick pay, paid holidays, health insurance, life insurance, and retirement programs.

WORK ENVIRONMENT

Aerospace engineers work in various settings depending on their job description. Those involved in research and design usually work in a traditional office setting. They spend considerable time at computers and drawing boards. Engineers involved with the testing of components and structures often work outside at test sites or in laboratories where controlled testing conditions can be created.

In the manufacturing area of the aerospace industry, engineers often work on the factory floor itself, assembling components and making sure that they conform to design specifications. This job requires much walking around large production facilities, such as aircraft factories or spacecraft assembly plants.

Engineers are sometimes required to travel to other locations to consult with companies that make materials and other needed components. Others travel to remote test sites to observe and participate in flight testing.

Aerospace engineers are also employed with the Federal Aviation Administration and commercial airline companies. These engineers perform a variety of duties, including performance analysis and crash investigations. Companies that are involved with satellite communications need the expertise of aerospace engineers to better interpret the many aspects of the space environment and the problems involved with getting a satellite launched into space.

OUTLOOK

Employment in this field is expected to grow more slowly than the average for all occupations through 2014, according to the U.S. Department of Labor. Shrinking space program budgets, increased job efficiency, and the continuing wave of corporate downsizing have all combined to cut severely into the aerospace industry.

Nevertheless, the aerospace industry remains vital to the health of the national economy. Increasing airline traffic and the need to replace aging airplanes with quieter and more fuel-efficient aircraft will boost demand for aerospace engineers. The federal government has increased defense budgets in order to build up the armed forces. More aerospace engineers will be needed to repair and add to the current air fleet, as well as to improve defense technology. Engineers are also needed to help make commercial aircraft safer, designing and installing reinforced cockpit doors and onboard security screening equipment to protect pilots, crew, and commercial passengers.

Despite cutbacks in the space program, the development of new space technology and increasing commercial uses for that technology will continue to require qualified engineers. Facing reduced demand in the United States, aerospace companies are increasing their sales overseas, and depending on the world economy and foreign demand, this new market could create a demand for new workers in the industry.

Even though the outlook for growth in this field is not especially favorable, graduates of aerospace engineering programs are highly sought after, since this field experienced a drop-off in graduates for several years due to perceived lack of job opportunities. With the right skills, talents, and determination, one can still find a promising career in this branch of engineering.

FOR MORE INFORMATION

For a list of accredited schools and colleges, contact
Accreditation Board for Engineering and Technology Inc.
111 Market Place, Suite 1050
Baltimore, MD 21202-7116
Tel: 410-347-7700
http://www.abet.org

For career information and details on student branches of this organization, contact
American Institute of Aeronautics and Astronautics
1801 Alexander Bell Drive, Suite 500
Reston, VA 20191-4344
Tel: 800-639-2422
http://www.aiaa.org

For information on educational programs and to purchase a copy of Engineering: Go For It, *contact*
American Society for Engineering Education
1818 N Street, NW, Suite 600
Washington, DC 20036-2479
Tel: 202-331-3500
http://www.asee.org

The following organization offers information geared specifically toward students:
Junior Engineering Technical Society
1420 King Street, Suite 405
Alexandria, VA 22314-2794
Tel: 703-548-5387
Email: info@jets.org
http://www.jets.org

For information on licensure and practice areas, contact
National Society of Professional Engineers
1420 King Street
Alexandria, VA 22314-2794
Tel: 703-684-2800
http://www.nspe.org/students

For information on aerospace programs and summer camps, contact
University of North Dakota
John D. Odergard School of Aerospace Sciences
PO Box 9007
University & Tulane
Grand Forks, ND 58202-9007
Tel: 800-258-1525
http://www.aero.und.edu

Automotive Industry Workers

OVERVIEW

Automotive industry workers are the people who work in the parts production and assembly plants of automobile manufacturers. Their labor involves work from the smallest part to the completed automobiles. Automotive industry workers read specifications; design parts; build, maintain, and operate machinery and tools used to produce parts; and assemble the automobiles.

HISTORY

In our mobile society, it is difficult to imagine a time without automobiles. Yet just over 100 years ago, there were none. In the late 1800s, inventors were just beginning to tinker with the idea of a self-propelled vehicle. Early experiments used steam to power a vehicle's engine. Two German engineers developed the first internal combustion engine fueled by gasoline. Karl Benz finished the first model in 1885, and Gottlieb Daimler finished building a similar model in 1886. Others around the world had similar successes in the late 1800s and early 1900s. In these early days, no one imagined people would become so reliant on the automobile as a way of life. In 1898, there were 50 automobile manufacturing companies in the United States, a number that rose to 241 by 1908.

Early automobiles were expensive to make and keep in working order and could be used to travel only short distances; they were "toys" for those who had the time and money to tinker with them. One such person

QUICK FACTS

School Subjects
Mathematics
Technical/shop

Personal Skills
Following instructions
Mechanical/manipulative

Work Environment
Primarily indoors
Primarily one location

Minimum Education Level
High school diploma

Salary Range
$27,000 to $40,000 to $100,000

Certification or Licensing
Voluntary

Outlook
More slowly than the average

DOT
007, 620, 729, 806

GOE
08.02.01, 08.02.03

NOC
9482

O*NET-SOC
51-1011.00, 51-2031.00, 51-2041.00, 51-2091.00, 51-2092.00, 51-2099.00, 51-4011.00, 51-4041.00, 51-4121.00, 51-9197.00, 51-9199.00

was Henry Ford. He differed from others who had succeeded in building automobiles in that he believed the automobile could appeal to the general public if the cost of producing them were reduced. The Model A was first produced by the Ford Motor Company in small quantities in 1903. Ford made improvements to the Model A, and in October 1908, he found success with the more practical Model T. The Model T was the vehicle that changed Ford's fortune and would eventually change the world. It was a powerful car with a possible speed of 45 miles per hour that could run 13 to 21 miles on a gallon of gasoline. Such improvements were made possible by the use of vanadium steel, a lighter and more durable steel than that previously used. Automobiles were beginning to draw interest from the general public as newspapers reported early successes, but they were still out of reach for most Americans. The automobile remained a curiosity to be read about in the newspapers until 1913. That's when Ford changed the way his workers produced automobiles in the factory. Before 1913, skilled craftsmen made automobiles in Ford's factory, but Ford's moving assembly line reduced the skill level needed and sped up production. The moving assembly line improved the speed of chassis assembly from 12 hours and eight minutes to one hour and 33 minutes. Craftsmen were no longer needed to make the parts and assemble the automobiles. Anyone could be trained for most of the jobs required to build an automobile in one of Ford's factories, making it possible to hire unskilled workers at lower wages.

For many early automotive workers, Ford's mass production concept proved to be both a blessing and a curse. Demand was growing for the affordable automobile, even during the Depression years, bringing new jobs for people who desperately needed them. However, working on an assembly line could be tedious and stressful at the same time. Ford paid his workers well (he introduced the $5 day in 1914, a high wage for the time), but he demanded a lot of them. He sped up the assembly line on several occasions, and many workers performed the same task for hours at a frenzied pace, often without a break.

Such conditions led workers to organize unions and, through the years, workers have gained more control over the speed at which they work and pay rates. Many of today's automotive industry workers belong to unions such as the United Auto Workers (founded in 1936). The industry continued to evolve with automotive technology in the 1940s and 1950s. American automobiles were generally large and consumed a lot of gasoline, but a strong U.S. economy afforded many Americans the ability to buy and maintain such vehicles. In Europe and Japan, smaller, fuel-efficient cars were more popular. This allowed foreign automakers to cut deeply into the American automobile market during fuel shortages in the 1970s. Automotive workers suffered job cuts in the 1980s because of declining exports and domestic sales.

Automotive industry workers must have the physical capability to stand for long periods, lift heavy objects, and maneuver hand tools and machinery. *(Jim West, The Image Works)*

Today, the industry has recovered from the losses of the 1980s largely by producing vehicles that can compete with fuel-efficient, foreign-made ones. Also, trade agreements have encouraged foreign automakers to build manufacturing plants in the United States, creating new jobs for U.S. workers. The United States currently has about one-quarter of the world's automobiles, some 128 million vehicles.

THE JOB

The term "automotive industry worker" covers the wide range of people who build the 5 million cars—about 14 percent of the world's total—produced in the United States each year. Automotive industry workers are employed in two types of plants: parts production plants and assembly plants. Similar jobs are also found with companies that manufacture farm and earth-moving equipment; their workers often belong to the same unions and undergo the same training. Major automobile manufacturers are generally organized so that automobiles are assembled at a few large plants that employ several thousand workers. Parts for the automobiles are made at smaller plants that may employ fewer than 100 workers. Some plants that produce parts are not owned by the automobile manufacturer but may be independent companies that specialize in making one important part. These independent manufacturers may supply parts to several different automobile makers.

Whether they work in a parts plant or an assembly plant, automotive workers are generally people who work with their hands, spend a lot of time standing, bending, and lifting, and do a lot of repetitive work. They often work in noisy areas and are required to wear protective equipment throughout their workday, such as safety glasses, earplugs, gloves, and masks. Because automotive industry workers often work in large plants that operate 24 hours a day, they usually work in shifts. Shift assignments are generally made on the basis of seniority.

Precision metalworker is one of the more highly skilled positions found in automotive production plants. Precision metalworkers create the metal tools, dies, and special guiding and holding devices that produce automotive parts—thus, they are sometimes called *tool and die makers*. They must be familiar with the entire manufacturing process and have knowledge of mathematics, blueprint reading, and the properties of metals, such as hardness and heat tolerance. Precision metalworkers may perform all or some of the steps needed to make machining tools, including reading blueprints, planning the sequence of operations, marking the materials, and cutting and assembling the materials into a tool. Precision metalworkers often work in quieter parts of the production plants.

Machinists make the precision metal parts needed for automobiles using tools such as lathes, drill presses, and milling machines. In automotive production plants, their work is repetitive as they generally produce large quantities of one part. Machinists may spend their entire shift machining the part. Some machinists also read blueprints or written specifications for a part. They calculate where to cut into the metal, how fast to feed the metal into the machine, or how much of the metal to remove. Machinists select tools and materials needed for the job and mark the metal stock for the cuts to be made. Increasingly, the machine tools used to make automotive parts are computerized. Computer numerically controlled machining is widespread in many manufacturing processes today. *Tool programmers* write the computer programs that direct the machine's operations, and machinists monitor the computer-controlled process.

Maintenance workers is a general category that refers to a number of jobs. Maintenance workers may repair or make new parts for existing machines. They also may set up new machines. They may work with sales representatives from the company that sold the automobile manufacturer the piece of equipment. Maintenance workers are responsible for the upkeep of machines and should be able to perform all of the machine's operations.

Welders use equipment that joins metal parts by melting and fusing them to form a permanent bond. There are different types of welds as well as equipment to make the welds. In manual welding, the work is controlled entirely by the welder. Other work is semiautomatic, in which machinery such as a wire feeder is used to help perform the weld. Much of the welding work in automotive plants is repetitive; in some of these cases, *welding machine operators* monitor machines as they perform the welding tasks. Because they work with fire, welders must wear safety gear, such as protective clothing, safety shoes, goggles, and hoods with protective lenses.

Inspectors check the manufacturing process at all stages to make sure products meet quality standards. Everything from raw materials to parts to the finished automobile is checked for dimensions, color, weight, texture, strength, and other physical characteristics, as well as proper operation. Inspectors identify and record any quality problems and may work with any of several departments to remedy the flaw. Jobs for inspectors are declining because inspection has become automated at many stages of production. Also, there is a move to have workers self-check their work on the production line.

Floor or line supervisors are responsible for a group of workers who produce one part or perform one step in a process. They may report to department heads or foremen who oversee several such departments. Many supervisors are production workers who have worked their way up the ranks; still others have a management background and, in many cases, a college degree in business or management.

REQUIREMENTS
High School
Many automotive industry jobs require mechanical skills, so you should take advantage of any shop programs your high school offers, such as auto mechanics, electronics, welding, drafting,

---

Books to Read

Aspatore Books Staff. *Inside the Minds: The Automotive Industry—Industry Leaders Share Their Knowledge on the Future of the Automotive World.* Boston: Aspatore Books, 2003.

Becker, Helmut. *High Noon in the Automotive Industry.* New York: Springer Publishing Company, 2006.

Braess, Hans-Hermann, and Ulrich Seiffert, eds. *Handbook Of Automotive Engineering.* Warrendale, Pa.: SAE International, 2005.

Kimes, Beverly R. *Pioneers, Engineers, and Scoundrels: The Dawn of the Automobile in America.* Warrendale, Pa.: SAE International, 2004.

Maxton, Graeme P., and John Wormald. *Time for a Model Change: Re-Engineering the Global Automotive Industry.* New York: Cambridge University Press, 2004.

and computer programming and design. In the core subject areas, mathematics, including algebra and geometry, is useful for reading blueprints and computer programs that direct machine functions. Chemistry is useful for workers who need to be familiar with the properties of metals. English classes are also important to help you communicate verbally with both supervisors and coworkers and to read and understand complex instructions.

Postsecondary Training

Many of the jobs in an automotive plant are classified as semiskilled or unskilled positions, and people with some mechanical aptitude, physical ability, and a high school diploma are qualified to do them. However, there is often stiff competition for jobs with large auto-makers like General Motors and Ford because they offer good bene-fits and pay compared to jobs that require similar skills. Therefore, if you have some postsecondary training, certification, or experience, you stand a better chance of getting a job in the automotive industry than someone with only a high school diploma.

Formal training for machining, welding, and toolmaking is offered in vocational schools, vocational-technical institutes, com-munity colleges, and private schools. Increasingly, such postsecond-ary training or certification is the route many workers take to getting an automotive industry job. In the past, apprenticeships and on-the-job training were the routes many workers took to get factory jobs, but these options are not as widely available today. Electricians, who generally must complete an apprenticeship, may find work in automotive plants as maintenance workers.

Certification or Licensing

Certification is available but not required for many of the positions in an automotive production plant. The American Welding Society offers several designations, including certified welding engineer and certified welding inspector to members who meet education and professional experience criteria as well as pass an examination. For precision metalworkers and machinists, the National Tooling and Machining Association operates training centers and apprentice pro-grams and sets skill standards.

Other Requirements

Working in an automotive production plant can be physically chal-lenging. For many jobs, you need the ability to stand for long peri-ods, lift heavy objects, and maneuver hand tools and machinery. However, a person with a physical disability can perform some of the jobs in an automotive production plant. For example, a person who uses a wheelchair may work well on an assembly line job that requires only the use of his or her hands. Automotive workers should have hand and finger dexterity and the ability to do repetitive work accurately and safely.

EXPLORING

Do you enjoy working with your hands? Following complex instructions? Do you think you could do repetitive work on a daily basis? Are you a natural leader who would enjoy a supervisory position? Once you have an idea what area of the automotive industry you want to pursue, the best way to learn more is to find someone who does the job and ask him or her questions about the work. Assembly plants are generally located in or near large cities, but if you live in a rural area you can still probably find someone with a similar job at a parts plant or other manufacturer. Even small towns generally have machine shops or other types of manufacturing plants that employ machinists, tool and die makers, inspectors, and other production workers. Local machine shops or factories are a good place to get experience, perhaps through a summer or after-school job to see if you enjoy working in a production environment. Many high schools have cooperative programs that employ students who want to gain work experience.

EMPLOYERS

Automotive industry workers can find jobs with both domestic automakers and with foreign automakers like Mitsubishi and Honda, which both have large assembly plants in the United States. Large assembly plants may employ several thousand workers. Parts production plants may employ fewer workers, but there are more of these plants. Assembly plants are generally located in or near large cities, especially in the Northeast and Midwest where heavy manufacturing is concentrated. Parts production plants vary in size, from a few dozen workers to several hundred. Employees of these plants may all work on one small part or on several parts that make up one component of an automobile. Parts production plants are located in smaller towns as well as urban areas. The production processes in agricultural and earth-moving equipment factories are similar to those in the automotive industry, and workers trained in welding, toolmaking, machining, and maintenance may find jobs with companies like Caterpillar and John Deere.

Approximately 1.1 million workers are employed in the industry, according to the U.S. Bureau of Labor Statistics—making it one of the largest manufacturing industries. The United Auto Workers

Union, the largest union in the industry, currently reports 640,000 active members.

STARTING OUT

Hiring practices at large plants are usually very structured. Such large employers generally don't place "help wanted" ads. Rather, they accept applications year-round and keep them on file. Applicants generally complete an initial application and may be placed on a hiring list. Others get started by working as temporary or part-time workers at the plant and using their experience and contacts to obtain full-time, permanent positions. Some plants work with career services offices of vocational schools and technical associations to find qualified workers. Others may recruit workers at job fairs. Also, as with many large factories, people who have a relative or know someone who works at the plant usually have a better chance of getting hired. Their contact may put in a good word with a supervisor or advise them when an opening occurs.

New hires are usually expected to join the United Auto Workers (UAW) or another union. Unions help negotiate with manufacturers and deal with the company on a worker's behalf.

ADVANCEMENT

Automotive production plants are very structured in their paths of advancement. Large human resources departments oversee the personnel structures of all departments; each job has a specific description with specific qualifications. Union rules and contracts further structure advancement. Longevity is usually the key to advancement in an automotive plant. For many, advancement means staying in the same position and moving up on the salary scale. Others acquire experience and further training to advance to a position with a higher skill level, more responsibility, and higher pay. For example, machinists may learn a lot about many different machines throughout their careers and may undergo training or be promoted to become precision metalworkers. Others with years of experience become supervisors of their departments.

EARNINGS

Salaries vary widely for automotive industry workers depending on their job and how long they've been with the company. Supervisors may earn $60,000 to $75,000 a year or more, depending on the number of people they supervise. Pay for semiskilled or unskilled workers, such as assemblers, is considerably lower, usually in the $27,000 range. Still, these production jobs are sought after because the pay is higher than that which workers may find elsewhere based on their skill level. The U.S. Department of Labor reports the following 2005 mean annual earnings for workers specializing in the production of motor vehicles, parts, and related equipment: first-line managers, $50,350; team assemblers, $41,560; machinists, $38,300; and welders, $28,650. Earnings are usually much higher for workers who are members of a union and employed by a Big Three automaker (General Motors, Ford, or Chrysler). Few of these workers earn less than $40,000 a year, and some earn as much as $100,000 a year because of mandatory overtime and six- or seven-day workweeks.

Workers employed by large, unionized companies such as Ford enjoy good benefits, including paid health insurance, paid holidays, sick days, and personal days. Large employers generally offer retirement plans and many match workers' contributions to retirement funds. Automotive industry workers who work for independent parts manufacturers may not enjoy the comprehensive benefit programs that employees of large companies do, but generally are offered health insurance and paid personal days.

WORK ENVIRONMENT

Working as a production worker in an automotive plant can be stressful, depending on the worker's personality, job duties, and management expectations. Assembly line workers have little control over the speed at which they must complete their work. They can generally take breaks only when scheduled. Norm Ritchie, a machine operator at a Chrysler parts plant in Perrysburg, Ohio, says the job can be stressful: "The pressure [of the assembly line] affects people in different ways. Sometimes people get pretty stressed out; other people can handle it." Ritchie, who works on steering shafts, also says that noise is a concern in his area of the plant. He estimates that the noise level is about 90 decibels all the time. Automotive production workers must follow several safety precautions every day, including wearing protective gear (such as earplugs) and undergoing safety training throughout their careers.

OUTLOOK

Only a small amount of job growth is expected for the U.S. automotive industry for the next few years. The U.S. Department of Labor predicts employment growth of only 2 percent in motor vehicle manufacturing, 6 percent in motor vehicle parts manufacturing, and 8 percent in motor vehicle body and trailer manufacturing—all much lower than the 14 percent growth predicted for all U.S. industries.

Economic downturns and rising fuel prices could cause production slowdowns (especially for larger American-made cars with poor gas mileage) and subsequent layoffs for auto industry workers, particularly those who work for American manufacturers. Many manufacturers have also found it more cost-effective to move operations overseas, where unions are weak and labor is cheaper. However, the decline in employment among American-owned automakers has been balanced by new foreign-owned manufacturing plants that have been built in the United States. Today, many U.S. automotive workers are employed by foreign-owned automakers such as Honda and Mitsubishi.

FOR MORE INFORMATION

These professional societies promote the skills of their trades and can provide career information.

American Welding Society
550 Lejeune Road, NW
Miami, FL 33126-5699
Tel: 800-443-9353
Email: info@aws.org
http://www.aws.org

National Tooling and Machining Association
9300 Livingston Road
Fort Washington, MD 20744-4914
Tel: 800-248-6862
http://www.ntma.org

These are two of many unions that represent automotive production workers. They can provide information about training and education programs in your area.

International Association of Machinists and Aerospace Workers
9000 Machinists Place
Upper Marlboro, MD 20772-2687
Tel: 301-967-4500
http://www.iamaw.org

United Auto Workers
8000 East Jefferson Avenue
Detroit, MI 48214-3963
Tel: 313-926-5000
http://www.uaw.org

Cost Estimators

OVERVIEW

Cost estimators use standard estimating techniques to calculate the cost of a construction or manufacturing project. They help contractors, owners, and project planners determine how much a project or product will cost to decide if it is economically viable. There are approximately 198,000 cost estimators employed in the United States.

HISTORY

Cost estimators collect and analyze information on various factors influencing costs, such as the labor, materials, and machinery needed for a particular project. Cost estimating became a profession as production techniques became more complex. Weighing the many costs involved in a construction or manufacturing project soon required specialized knowledge beyond the skills and training of the average builder or contractor. Today, cost estimators work in many industries but are predominantly employed in construction and manufacturing.

THE JOB

QUICK FACTS

School Subjects
Business
Economics
Mathematics

Personal Skills
Leadership/management
Technical/scientific

Work Environment
Indoors and outdoors
Primarily multiple locations

Minimum Education Level
Some postsecondary training

Salary Range
$31,600 to $52,940 to $88,310+

Certification or Licensing
Recommended

Outlook
Faster than the average

DOT
160

GOE
13.02.04

NOC
2234

O*NET-SOC
13-1051.00

In the construction industry, the nature of the work is largely determined by the type and size of the project being estimated. For a large building project, for example, the estimator reviews architectural drawings and other bidding documents before any construction begins. The estimator then visits the potential construction site to collect information that may affect the way the structure is built, such as the site's access to transportation, water, electricity, and other needed resources. While out in the field, the estimator also analyzes the topography of the land, taking note of its general characteristics, such as drainage areas and the location of trees and other vegetation. After compiling thorough research, the estimator writes a quantity survey, or takeoff. This is an itemized report of the quantity of materials and labor a firm will need for the proposed project.

Large projects often require several estimators, all specialists in a given area. For example, one estimator may assess the electrical costs of a project, while another concentrates on the transportation or insurance costs. In this case, it is the responsibility of a *chief estimator* to combine the reports and submit one development proposal.

In manufacturing, estimators work with engineers to review blueprints and other designs. They develop a list of the materials and labor needed for production. Aiming to control costs but maintain quality, estimators must weigh the option of producing parts in-house or purchasing them from other vendors. After this research, they write a report on the overall costs of manufacturing, taking into consideration influences such as improved employee learning curves, material waste, overhead, and the need to correct problems as manufacturing goes along.

To write their reports, estimators must know current prices for labor and materials and other factors that influence costs. They obtain this data through commercial price books, catalogs, and the Internet or by calling vendors directly to obtain quotes.

Estimators should also be able to compute and understand accounting and mathematical formulas in order to make their cost reports. Computer programs are frequently used to do the routine calculations, producing more accurate results and leaving the estimator with more time to analyze data.

REQUIREMENTS
High School
To prepare for a job in cost estimating, you should take courses in accounting, business, economics, and mathematics. Because a large part of this job involves comparing calculations, it is essential that you are comfortable and confident with your math skills. English courses with a heavy concentration in writing are also recommended to develop your communication skills. Cost estimators must be able to write clear and accurate reports of their analyses. Finally, drafting and shop courses are also useful since estimators must be able to review and understand blueprints and other design plans.

Postsecondary Training

Though not required for the job, most employers of cost estimators in both construction and manufacturing prefer applicants with formal education. In construction, cost estimators generally have associate's or bachelor's degrees in construction management, construction science, engineering, or architecture. Those employed with manufacturers often have degrees in physical science, business, mathematics, operations research, statistics, engineering, economics, finance, or accounting.

Many colleges and universities offer courses in cost estimating as part of the curriculum for an associate's, bachelor's, or master's degree. These courses cover subjects such as cost estimating, cost control, project planning and management, and computer applications. The Association for the Advancement of Cost Engineering International offers a list of education programs related to cost engineering. Visit its Web site, http://www.aacei.org, for more information.

Certification or Licensing

Although it is not required, many cost estimators find it helpful to become certified to improve their standing within the professional community. Obtaining certification proves that the estimator has obtained adequate job training and education. Information on certification procedures is available from organizations such as the American Society of Professional Estimators, the Association for the Advancement of Cost Engineering International, and the Society of Cost Estimating and Analysis.

Other Requirements

To be a cost estimator, you should have sharp mathematical and analytical skills. Cost estimators must work well with others, and be confident and assertive when presenting findings to engineers, business owners, and design professionals. To work as a cost estimator in the construction industry, you will likely need some experience before you start, which can be gained through an internship or cooperative education program.

EXPLORING

Practical work experience is necessary to become a cost estimator. Consider taking a part-time position with a construction crew or manufacturing firm during your summer vacations. Because of more favorable working conditions, construction companies are busiest during the summer months and may be looking for additional assistance. Join any business or manufacturing clubs that your school may offer.

Another way to discover more about career opportunities is simply by talking to a professional cost estimator. Ask your school counselor to help arrange an interview with an estimator to ask questions about his or her job demands, work environment, and personal opinion of the job.

EMPLOYERS

Approximately 198,000 cost estimators are employed in the United States: 58 percent by the construction industry and 17 percent by manufacturing companies. Other employers include engineering and architecture firms, business services, the government, and a wide range of other industries.

Estimators are employed throughout the country, but the largest concentrations are found in cities or rapidly growing suburban areas. More job opportunities exist in or near large commercial or government centers.

STARTING OUT

Cost estimators often start out working in the industry as laborers, such as construction workers. After gaining experience and taking the necessary training courses, a worker may move into the more specialized role of estimator. Another possible route into cost estimating is through a formal training program, either through a professional organization that sponsors educational programs or through technical schools, community colleges, or universities. School career services counselors can be good sources of employment leads for recent graduates. Applying directly to manufacturers, construction firms, and government agencies is another way to find your first job.

Whether employed in construction or manufacturing, most cost estimators are provided with intensive on-the-job training. Generally, new hires work with experienced estimators to become familiar with the work involved. They develop skills in blueprint reading and learn construction specifications before accompanying estimators to the construction site. In time, new hires learn how to determine quantities and specifications from project designs and report appropriate material and labor costs.

ADVANCEMENT

Promotions for cost estimators are dependent on skill and experience. Advancement usually comes in the form of more responsibility and higher wages. A skilled cost estimator at a large construction company may become a chief estimator. Some experienced cost estimators go into consulting work, offering their services to government, construction, and manufacturing firms.

EARNINGS

Salaries vary according to the size of the construction or manufacturing firm and the experience and education of the worker. According to the U.S. Department of Labor, the median annual salary for cost estimators was $52,940 in 2006. The lowest 10 percent earned less than $31,600 and the highest 10 percent earned more than $88,310. Starting salaries for graduates of engineering or construction management programs were higher than those with degrees in other fields. A salary survey by the National Association of Colleges and Employers reports that candidates with degrees in construction science/management were offered average starting salaries of $42,923 a year in 2005.

WORK ENVIRONMENT

Much of the cost estimator's work takes place in a typical office setting with access to accounting records and other information. However, estimators must also visit construction sites or manufacturing facilities to inspect production procedures. These sites may be dirty, noisy, and potentially hazardous if the cost estimator is not equipped with proper protective gear such as a hard hat or earplugs. During a site visit, cost estimators consult with engineers, work supervisors, and other professionals involved in the production or manufacturing process.

Estimators usually work a 40-hour week, although longer hours may be required if a project faces a deadline. For construction estimators, overtime hours almost always occur in the summer when most projects are in full force.

OUTLOOK

Employment for cost estimators is expected to increase faster than the average for all occupations through 2014, according to the U.S. Department of Labor. As in most industries, highly trained college graduates and those with the most experience will have the best job prospects.

Many jobs will arise from the need to replace workers leaving the industry, either to retire or change jobs. In addition, growth within the residential and commercial construction industry creates much of the employment demand for estimators. The fastest growing areas in construction are in special trade and government projects, including the building and repairing of highways, streets, bridges, subway systems, airports, water and sewage systems, and electric power plants and transmission lines. Additionally, opportunities will be good in residential and school construction, as well as in the construction of nursing and extended care facilities. Cost estimators with degrees in construction management or in construction science, engineering, or architecture will have the best employment prospects. In manufacturing, employment is predicted to remain stable, though growth is not expected to be as strong as in construction. Estimators will be in demand because employers will continue to need their services to control operating costs. Estimators with degrees in engineering, science, mathematics, business administration, or economics will have the best employment prospects in this industry.

FOR MORE INFORMATION

For information on certification and educational programs, contact
American Society of Professional Estimators
2525 Perimeter Place Drive, Suite 103
Nashville, TN 37214-3674
Tel: 888-EST-MATE
Email: info@aspenational.com
http://www.aspenational.com

For information on certification, educational programs, and scholarships, contact
Association for the Advancement of Cost Engineering International
209 Prairie Avenue, Suite 100
Morgantown, WV 26501-5934
Tel: 800-858-2678
Email: info@aacei.org
http://www.aacei.org

For information on certification, job listings, and a glossary of cost-estimating terms, visit the SCEA Web site:
Society of Cost Estimating and Analysis (SCEA)
527 Maple Avenue East, Suite 301
Vienna, VA 22180-4753
Tel: 703-938-5090
Email: scea@sceaonline.net
http://www.sceaonline.net

INTERVIEW

Richard Coleman is a cost estimator and is the director of the Cost and Pricing Center of Excellence at Northrop Grumman, a global defense and technology company. He discussed his career with the editors of Careers in Focus: Manufacturing.

Q. How long have you been a cost estimator?

A. I have been a cost estimator since 1990, although I have a degree in operations research and so have worked in related fields since 1977. I work in Northern Virginia (specifically Chantilly, Virginia).

Q. Why did you decide to become a cost estimator?

A. As a navy captain, I was assigned a position as director for the Navy Center for Cost Analysis, based upon my degree, in 1990, and I stayed in the field after that. I stayed because I found the work challenging, fun, and intellectually rewarding, as well as being important to the country.

Q. Please take us through a day in your life as a cost estimator. What are your typical tasks/responsibilities?

A. I am quite senior, so my activities are not typical. I travel by air an average of 25 times per year to cities such as Los Angeles, California; New Orleans, Louisiana; Newport News, Virginia; Orlando, Florida; Melbourne, Florida; and others in the line of work. I spend about 50 percent of my time in overhead work, and 50 percent on direct projects. The direct work usually involves independent cost evaluations of big proposals for my company. I have been the lead of evaluations for two aircraft carriers, destroyers, amphibious ships, a large number of information technology programs, and a few classified programs in the intelligence community. These programs routinely cost between $100 million and $5 billion. I routinely lead small-to-medium teams in short-duration evaluations that last one to four weeks. I also work on a few government programs for the navy and the intelligence community.

Cost estimators tend to work in [company] headquarters and are particularly numerous in industries involving defense and government contracts and at the government agencies that oversee these manufacturers. They are most numerous in northern Virginia, Washington, D.C., and Maryland. Cost estimators are involved in the determination, by statistical and analytical techniques, of the number of labor hours and the quantity of material needed. Pricers, by contrast, apply rates to labor hours and apply bid prices to bid bills of materials and so are more evenly distributed across the country in clusters where the headquarters and major manufacturing facilities are found.

Q. What advice would you give to high school students who are interested in this career?

A. Math and statistics are important, as well as science classes (science and engineering principles underlie the discipline). Don't keep asking, "Why should I take this class? I'll never use it." You will; the course work in high school is well chosen for future applicability, and you will use these courses if you continue to succeed. Sports, at an appropriate level, will also serve you well, particularly team sports, as they are excellent preparation for workforce relationships and dynamics.

Q. What is the future employment outlook in the field?

A. The field of cost analysis (estimation) is a niche field for which good candidates are hard to find. If you become a cost estimator, you will always have work—it's a lifetime opportunity! I have a much broader degree, with a bachelor of science from the U.S. Naval Academy and a master of science from the Naval Postgraduate School, but when I retired I quickly discovered that this field was rewarding and wide open.

Glass Manufacturing Workers

OVERVIEW

There are approximately 108,000 *glass manufacturing workers* in the United States, employed in factories and plants that make glass and glass products from raw materials. These products include flat glass, such as window and plate glass; pressed glass items, such as glass dishes; blown glass items, such as light bulbs and many kinds of bottles; and various special products, such as glass blocks used in building construction, safety glass windshields, and glass for optical instruments.

HISTORY

People have been manufacturing glass for about 4,500 years. The earliest glass objects were produced taking little advantage of the special qualities of hot glass. A major advance came around 200 B.C., when techniques were devised (probably in Syria) for blowing air into gobs of molten glass to shape the glass into useful objects. The new knowledge about working with hot glass spread quickly among glassmakers, and soon other peoples, notably the Romans, were making blown glass items. With the decline of Rome, much of the knowledge of working with glass was lost, not to be revived until glassworkers in Venice created a thriving industry around the 13th century. For hundreds of years, Venice was the leading center of glass production. In time, Venetian methods spread, new kinds of glass were developed, and good-quality blown glass was produced across much of Europe.

Skilled glassmakers were among the early European colonists in North America. However, not until the 18th century did glassmaking

QUICK FACTS

School Subjects
Chemistry
Technical/shop

Personal Skills
Mechanical/manipulative
Technical/scientific

Minimum Education Level
High school diploma

Salary Range
$30,000 to $35,000 to $40,000+

Certification or Licensing
None available

Outlook
About as fast as the average

DOT
772

GOE
01.06.01

NOC
9413

O*NET-SOC
51-9021.00, 51-9022.00, 51-9031.00, 51-9032.03, 51-9051.00, 51-9195.04

become a successful industry in the United States. Even at that time, glass was still made by hand and was so difficult to produce that it was expensive and seldom found in poor homes. In the 19th century, a steady stream of technological innovations simplified the various methods of production and made glass much more common. More efficient furnaces melted raw materials much faster; new molds made bottles much easier to mass produce; improved methods simplified the production of flat glass; and better polishing equipment greatly increased the output of plate glass for windows, creating a new look in buildings.

Major advances in the scientific understanding of glass and its properties have brought changes in manufacturing processes and new applications for glass products. Many new types of glass, such as heat-resistant glass, glass fabrics, and laminated glass, have been introduced. Although some craftworkers and artists still follow the old ways of making glass by hand, most modern glass is made in factories that use highly organized, automated industrial processes.

THE JOB

Glass manufacturing involves a number of basic operations, including mixing and melting materials; forming molten glass by blowing, pressing, casting, drawing, or rolling; heat-conditioning and controlled cooling; and finishing glass by polishing, coating, and using other surface processes. Different kinds of glass may involve different processes and require specialized workers. Most of today's glass manufacturing workers tend to specialized machines used as part of a continuous mechanized operation.

Glass is usually made from sand (silicon dioxide), limestone (calcium carbonate), soda ash (sodium carbonate), and other raw ingredients. In many plants where glass is made, mixers tend equipment that blends ingredients. They either weigh and mix batches of materials or monitor machines that automatically supply the correct mix for melting in furnaces. *Cullet crushers* tend machines that crush and wash cullet, or broken waste glass, which will be recycled and melted with the raw ingredients. In some plants, *batch-and-furnace operators* control automatic equipment that can weigh and mix ingredients, then dump them into a furnace. *Combustion analysts* test and regulate the temperature of the furnace to manufacturing specifications. When the temperature is properly controlled, bubbles and impurities can be eliminated.

Many workers are concerned with machine-forming of the hot glass so they can take advantage of glass's malleable quality. Among these workers are *forming machine operators*, who set up and operate machines that press, blow, or spin lumps of molten glass into molds to make a wide variety of glass products, such as bottles, containers, and cathode-ray tubes. Under operator control, the machines deliver gobs of hot glass from the supply emerging from the furnace. Often, a puff of air is used to blow the glass firmly into a mold. The glass temperature is regulated until the molded item is ejected for further processing. *Pressers* tend press molds that force molten glass into shapes, making cast glassware items such as plates and automobile headlights. Others tend machines that extrude fiberglass filaments, mold optical glass blanks, form bulbs, and shape other glass products.

Flat glass is an extremely important product for windows, doors, and many other items. The float-glass process is used to produce much of the flat glass made today. In this process, molten glass flows from the furnace where it has been heated onto the surface of a pool of molten tin. The result is a glass with a good polish and flatness that requires less costly finish processing than other flat glass.

The glass manufacturing workers who make flat glass by other methods include *drawing-kiln operators,* who operate machines that process molten glass into continuous sheets by drawing molten glass upward from a tank and cooling it before it runs and loses its shape. Sometimes sheets of glass are made by *rolling-machine operators,* who operate equipment that rolls molten glass flat.

A worker operates machinery in a glass manufacturing factory. (*John Birdsall, The Image Works*)

Some workers form hot glass by hand. They include *glassblowers,* who shape gobs of molten glass into glassware by blowing through a blowpipe, in much the same way that glass has been blown for centuries. Glassblowers produce certain kinds of special scientific equipment, as well as unique tableware and art objects. Other craftworkers shape and attach hot glass to other objects to make handles and pedestals.

Some glass is further processed with controlled reheating and slow cooling to eliminate flaws and internal stresses. *Lehr tenders* operate lehrs, which are tunnel-like automatic ovens used to heat-treat flat glass and glassware and fuse painted designs on glass.

Many glass products are not complete until they have been given other finishing treatments. Among the workers who do these tasks are *glass decorators,* who etch or cut designs into the surface of glass articles. *Glass grinders* remove rough edges and surface irregularities from glassware using belt or disk grinders. *Polishers* polish the edges and surfaces of flat glass, using polishing wheels.

REQUIREMENTS

High School

Many workers in glass manufacturing occupations, such as machine tenders, can be hired as inexperienced beginners and learn the skills they need on the job. If you plan to work in glass manufacturing, a good background includes high school courses in shop, general mathematics, and applied sciences. A high school diploma is not required, but many employers often prefer candidates that have graduated or at least have a general equivalency diploma.

Postsecondary Training

Apprenticeship programs are recommended for training skilled glassmaking workers. These programs combine on-the-job training with formal instruction in related fields. Some apprenticeships are sponsored and run by local joint union-employer committees or by large glass manufacturing firms. The content of the training programs may vary somewhat, but programs usually last about three years. An example is the program of the Glass, Molders, Pottery, Plastics and Allied Workers International Union, which involves on-the-job work experience as well as classroom study.

Other Requirements

Because they work mostly with automated processes, glass manufacturing workers usually need only enough strength to lift light-

or medium-weight objects. They must be able to tolerate repetitive work yet maintain careful attention to what they are doing while they oversee the operation of machines. Also, although union membership is not a requirement for employment (for example, most flat-glass workers do not belong to a union), many workers in the glass manufacturing industry are represented by a union, such as the Glass, Molders, Pottery, Plastics and Allied Workers International Union and the United Steel Workers of America Flint/Glass Industry Conference.

EXPLORING

If you are interested in making glassware, art and shop courses in high school will help you develop manual dexterity and learn about some of the tools and techniques used in glassmaking. Community art centers and adult education programs frequently offer classes in glassblowing, molding, and stained-glass construction. With the help of a teacher or guidance counselor, arrange to visit a glass manufacturing plant or a shop where artisans work with glass. One interesting field trip would take you to the Corning Museum of Glass at the Corning Glass Center in Corning, New York. The museum has more than 45,000 glass objects, from 3,500 years ago to the present; its library is the main research center for students of glass. And you can see a demonstration of actual glassblowing at the museum's Hot Glass Show.

EMPLOYERS

Approximately 108,000 glass manufacturing workers are employed in the United States. Most workers in glass manufacturing work in factories in or near big cities in many sections of the country, where they work with pressed or blown glass. Others work in plants making glass containers, and some work with flat glass. One of the world leaders in specialty glass materials is Corning, the company that supplied the glass for Thomas Edison's first light bulb and influenced the use of red, yellow, and green lights for traffic control. Among the applications for Corning's glass technology were the first mass-produced TV tubes, freezer-to-oven ceramic cookware, and car headlights. In the 1970s, Corning pioneered the development of optical fiber and auto emission technology; in 1993, the company was chosen by AT&T to provide fiber-optic couplers for its undersea telecommunications system and developed an electrically heated catalytic converter that could meet strict California emissions standards. The company is the world's number-one producer of tableware and cookware, led by its patented Pyrex and Corning Ware heat-resistant oven containers.

STARTING OUT

If you want an entry-level job in the glass manufacturing industry, you can apply directly to factories that may be hiring new workers. You might find leads to specific job openings through the classified ads in newspapers and the local offices of your state's employment service. Because many workers in this field are union members, it's a good idea to check out local union offices for job listings and general information about local opportunities.

If you want to be an apprentice in the industry, you might find information through union offices, glass manufacturing companies, and state services. After finishing your apprenticeship program, you could be rehired by the same company for which you apprenticed.

ADVANCEMENT

Advancement opportunities for glassworkers are similar to those in many other fields. Glass manufacturing workers who are disciplined, motivated, and reliable have the best chance for promotion and increased earnings. Glassworkers can be trained to operate many types of equipment, either through their company or with the help of their union. After they have gained some seniority and a diversity of glassmaking skills, glassworkers would be qualified to transfer to other jobs, shifts, or supervisory positions when they become available.

EARNINGS

Earnings of glass manufacturing workers depend on the type of industry they work in, their specific duties, union membership, the shift they work, and other factors. Production workers in flat-glass manufacturing average about $30,000 per year; those in pressed and blown glassmaking production jobs earn an average of $35,000 per year; those who produce glass containers average $34,000. Managers may earn $40,000 or more annually. Those who work more than eight hours a day or 40 hours per week receive overtime pay, and they are usually paid at higher rates if they work at night, on weekends, or on holidays.

Workers in many factories are union members, and their earnings are established according to agreements between the unions and company management. In addition, glassworkers often receive benefits, such as retirement plans and health and life insurance.

WORK ENVIRONMENT

Glass factories usually operate around the clock, 24 hours every day of the year, because the furnaces have to be kept going all the time. For this reason, many workers work at night, on weekends, and on holidays. Although the standard workweek is about 40 hours, many workers put in overtime hours on a regular basis.

Factory conditions in glass plants have greatly improved over the years. On the job, workers may have to contend with some heat and fumes, but for the most part ventilation and heat shielding in modern plants have reduced worker exposure to these factors to acceptable levels. Workers who tend furnaces and ovens are the most likely to work in hot conditions. Glass plants can be noisy, and workers may have to spend long periods of time on their feet.

OUTLOOK

Glass is so common in our lives that as long as we continue to use it in its myriad forms, workers in glass manufacturing will be needed. It is difficult to say with any accuracy, however, whether job growth will be fast or slow or will remain the same. Much of the environment in the glass industry depends on other industries that use glass, like automobiles, spacecraft, nuclear energy, electronics, and solar energy. There are two markets for which new developments may be more important than others and thus require new workers: switchable glass (in which the ability of the glass to be seen through is changed by electronic and other means) and glass used in energy conservation.

FOR MORE INFORMATION

The following is a museum and educational site that has more than 45,000 objects of glass on view, a comprehensive library on the art and history of glass, and a studio that offers classes for all skill levels.

Corning Museum of Glass
One Museum Way
Corning, NY 14830-2253
Tel: 800-732-6845

Email: education@cmog.org
http://www.cmog.org

The following union represents glass manufacturing workers.
Glass, Molders, Pottery, Plastics & Allied Workers International Union
608 East Baltimore Pike
PO Box 607
Media, PA 19063-0607
Tel: 610-565-5051
Email: gmpiu@gmpiu.org
http://www.gmpiu.org

This is a nonprofit trade association that represents the flat-glass industry and offers educational services, such as the Glass Management Institute.
National Glass Association
8200 Greensboro Drive, Suite 302
McLean, VA 22102-3881
Tel: 866-342-5642
http://www.glass.org

The following union represents glass manufacturing workers.
United Steel Workers of America Flint/Glass Industry Conference
Five Gateway Center
Pittsburgh, PA 15222-1214
Tel: 412-562-2400
http://www.uswa.org/uswa/program/content

For information on the glass industry, visit
Glasslinks.com
http://www.glasslinks.com

Industrial Chemicals Workers

OVERVIEW

Industrial chemicals workers are employed in a variety of interrelated and interdependent industries and companies in which one concern often makes chemical precursors or starting materials for another's use. Most chemical workers convert the starting products or raw materials into other chemical compounds and derivative products, such as pharmaceuticals, plastics, solvents, and paints. In addition to being actively engaged in chemical operations, some workers are required to maintain safety, health, and environmental standards mandated by the federal government and perform routine and preventive maintenance tasks. Still others handle, store, and transport chemicals and operate batch processes.

HISTORY

Although its origins can be traced back to ancient Greece, chemistry was recognized as a physical science during the 17th century. The alkali industry, which began then, made alkalis (caustic compounds such as sodium or potassium hydroxide) and alkaline salts such as soda ash (sodium carbonate) from wood and plant ashes. These compounds were then used to make soap and glass. By 1775, the natural sources of these alkaline compounds could not meet demand. Encouraged by the French Academy of Sciences, Nicholas Leblanc devised a synthetic process to manufacture them cheaply. Large-scale use of his process came a few years later in England. Inspired and encouraged by Leblanc's success, other scientists developed new methods for making a variety of industrially important chemicals. This marked the beginning of the modern industrial chemicals industry. In the 1880s, the Leblanc process was superseded by the Solvay process. In the industrial chemical field today, many compounds, such as ethylene, which is derived from petroleum, are used to synthesize countless other useful products. Ethylene can be used to make polyethylene, polyethylene terephthalate, polystyrene, vinyl plastics, ethyl alcohol, and ethyl ether, to name just a few. Many of these, in turn, are used in fibers, fabrics, paints, resins, fuels, and pharmaceuticals. Thus, it is evident how one industry feeds off and relies on another. New uses for chemicals continue to be found, as well as new compounds to be synthesized. Some of these compounds will eventually supplant those now in use.

THE JOB

Workers in industrial chemicals plants make all the products previously mentioned plus thousands more. Basic chemicals such as sulfuric acid, nitric acid, hydrochloric acid, sodium hydroxide, sodium chloride, and ammonia are made by giant companies. The demand for these products is so great that only large companies can afford to build the factories and buy the equipment and the raw materials to produce these chemicals at the low prices for which they sell them. On the other hand, these giant companies rarely make specialty chemicals because they either can't afford to or they don't wish to make the necessary investment due to the very limited market. Those products are made by small companies.

Because of the large variety of chemicals produced and the number of different processes involved, there are hundreds of job categories. Many of the jobs have quite a bit in common. In general, workers measure batches according to formulas; set reaction parameters for temperature, pressure, or flow of materials; and read gauges to monitor processes. They do routine testing, keep records, and may write progress reports. Many operators use computerized control panels to monitor processes. Some operate mixing machines, agitator tanks, blenders, steam cookers, and other equipment. The worker may pour two or more raw ingredients from storage vats into a reaction vessel or empty cars from overhead conveyors, dumping the contents of a barrel or drum, or manually transfer materials from a hopper, box, or other container. The worker measures a preset amount of ingredients and then activates the mixing machine, while keeping an eye on the gauges and controls.

When the mixture has reached the desired consistency, color, or other characteristic, a test sample may be removed. If the analysis is satisfactory, the mixture is moved to its next destination either by piping, pumping into another container or processing machine, emptying into drums or vats, or by a conveyor. The operator then records the amount and condition of the mixture and readies his equipment for the next run.

Other workers may separate contaminants, undesirable byproducts, and unreacted materials with equipment that filters, strains, sifts, or centrifuges. Filters and centrifuges are often used to separate a slurry into liquid and solid parts. The *filter-press operator* sets up the press by covering the filter plates with canvas or paper sheets that separate the solids from the liquid portion. After the filtration, the plates are removed and cleaned. The centrifuge is a machine that spins a solid-liquid mixture like a washing machine in the spin cycle to separate it into solid and liquid components. If the desired end product is the liquid, the *centrifuge operator* discards the solids, and vice versa.

Distillation operators use equipment that separates liquid mixtures by first heating them to their boiling points. The heated vapors rise into a distillation column. If a very pure liquid is desired, a fractional distillation column is used. A distillation apparatus consists of an electrically or steam-heated still pot, a distillation column, a water-cooled condenser, and a collector. In this process, the hot vapors rise through the distillation column. The condenser cools the vapors and converts them back into a liquid. The condensed liquid is collected and removed for further use. Distillation, a very important separation technique for purifying and separating liquids, is widely used in the liquor industry, petroleum refineries, and chemical companies that make and use liquid chemicals.

Solid chemical mixtures often need to be dried before they can be used. Workers heat, bake, dry, and melt chemicals with kilns, vacuum dryers, rotary or tunnel furnaces, and spray dryers. The workers who operate this equipment, regardless of the industry, perform the same operations.

The paint industry manufactures paints, varnishes, shellacs, lacquers, and a variety of liquid products for decorative and protective coatings. It not only makes many of the materials that go into its products but also purchases chemicals, resins, solvents, dyes, and pigments from others. In its operations, it performs many of the same tasks as those described. Coating and laminating are related industries. Their workers operate press rollers; laminating, coating, and printing machines; and sprayers. They carefully apply measured thicknesses of coating materials to a variety of substrates, such as paper, plastic, metal, and fabric.

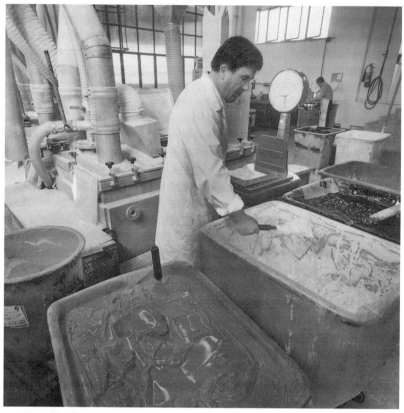

An industrial chemicals worker tests pigments at a manufacturing plant. *(Corbis)*

REQUIREMENTS

High School

Most of the equipment in the industrial chemicals industry is now automated and computer controlled. Because of the complex equipment used, employers prefer to hire workers with at least a high school diploma. Knowledge of basic mathematics, science, and computer skills is essential for those seeking employment in this field. Machine shop experience is also useful.

Postsecondary Training

Entry-level employees always get on-the-job training and special classroom work. Classes may include heat transfer principles, the basics of distillation, how to take readings on tanks and other equipment, and how to read blueprints. Workers also get safety training about the chemicals and processes they will encounter.

More advanced knowledge of chemistry and physics is important for those who hope to advance to supervisory and managerial positions. Training to become a skilled operator may take two to five years. Information on apprenticeship programs can be found through state employment bureaus. Some community colleges offer programs that allow students to combine classroom work with on-the-job experience to enhance their skills and knowledge.

Other Requirements

Workers in this industry must be dependable, alert, accurate, and able to follow instructions exactly. They must always be mindful of the potential hazards involved in working with chemicals and cannot ever be careless. They should be conscientious, able to work without direct supervision, willing to do repetitive and sometimes monotonous work, and be able to work well with others.

EXPLORING

A helpful and inexpensive way to explore employment opportunities is to talk with someone who has worked in the industry in which you are interested. Also, it may be possible to arrange a tour of a manufacturing plant by contacting its public relations department. Another way to explore chemical manufacturing occupations is to check high school or public libraries for books on the industry. Other sources include trade journals, high school guidance counselors, and university career services offices. You should join your high school or college science clubs. You can also subscribe to the American Chemical Society's *ChemMatters,* a quarterly magazine for high school chemistry students. (To read the magazine online, visit the society's Web site, http://www.chemistry.org/portal/a/c/s/1/home. html, and click "Educators and Students.")

EMPLOYERS

Industrial chemicals workers are a necessary part of all chemical manufacturing whether the industry is producing basic chemicals, pharmaceuticals, paints, food, or a myriad of other products. The companies that employ them vary in size, depending on the nature of the products they produce. Some large industrial chemicals companies (DuPont and Dow Chemical Company, for example) may make the chemicals they use in their own operations. Others purchase what they need from specialty chemical companies, such as Mallinckrodt Baker.

Basic chemicals, such as sodium hydroxide and nitric acid, are usually made by giant companies while small companies may make fine or specialty chemicals to supply to other manufacturers. Some workers are involved in the actual production process; others focus on the equipment used in manufacturing; still others test finished products to ensure that they meet industry and government standards of purity and safety. There are a number of government laboratories, such as the Department of Agriculture and the National Institute of Standards and Technology, that employ chemical workers.

STARTING OUT

High school graduates qualify for entry-level factory jobs as helpers, laborers, and material movers. They learn how to handle chemicals safely and acquire skills that enable them to advance to higher levels of responsibility. Students interested in a job in the industrial chemicals industry should look for information on job openings through classified ads and employment agencies. Information can also be obtained by contacting the personnel offices of individual chemical plants and local union offices of the International Chemical Workers Union and the United Steel, Paper and Forestry, Rubber, Manufacturing, Energy, Allied-Industrial and Service Workers International Union (more commonly known as the United Steelworkers of America). High school and college guidance and career services offices are other knowledgeable sources.

ADVANCEMENT

Movement into higher paying jobs is possible with increased experience and on-the-job training. Advancement usually requires mastery of advanced skills. Employers often offer classes for those who want to improve their skills and advance their careers.

Most workers start as laborers or unskilled helpers. They can advance to mechanic and installer jobs through formal vocational or in-house training. Or they can move up to positions as skilled operators of complex processes. They may become operators who monitor the flow and mix ratio of chemicals as they go through the production process. Experienced and well-trained production workers can advance to become supervisors overseeing an entire process.

EARNINGS

In 2005, median annual earnings for chemical equipment operators and tenders were $39,030, according to the U.S. Department of Labor. Chemical plant and system operators earned median annual salaries of $46,710, while mixing and blending machine setters, operators, and tenders averaged $28,890. Managers and supervisors earn salaries that range from $50,000 to $60,000 or higher, depending on job duties and the number of workers that they supervise. Workers are usually paid more for night, weekend, and overtime work. Hourly rates for each production job are often set by union contract. Fringe benefits vary among employers. They may include group, hospital, dental, and life insurance; paid holidays and vacations; and pension plans. Also, many workers qualify for college tuition aid from their companies.

WORK ENVIRONMENT

Working conditions in plants vary, depending on specific jobs, the type and condition of the equipment used, and the size and age of the plant. Chemical processing jobs used to be very dangerous, dirty, and disagreeable. However, working conditions have steadily improved over the years as a result of environmental, safety, and health standards mandated by the government. As a result of government intervention, chemical manufacturing now has an excellent safety record that is superior to other manufacturing industries. Nevertheless, chemical plants by their very nature can be extremely hazardous if strict safety procedures are not followed and enforced. Precautions include wearing protective clothing and equipment where required. Hard hats and safety goggles are worn throughout the plant.

Although few jobs in this industry are strenuous, they may become monotonous. Since manufacturing is a continuous process, most chemical plants operate around the clock. Once a process has begun, it cannot be stopped. This means that workers are needed for three shifts; split, weekend, and night shifts are common.

OUTLOOK

While the output and productivity of the industrial chemicals industry is expected to increase, the U.S. Department of Labor predicts that employment for industrial chemicals workers will decline through 2014. More efficient production processes, increased plant automation, and growing competition with overseas chemical manufacturers will limit job growth for production workers in this industry.

Advancing technology should create jobs for technical workers with the necessary skills to handle increasingly complex chemical processes and controls, as well as jobs for computer specialists who have technical expertise in computer-controlled production.

FOR MORE INFORMATION

To subscribe to ChemMatters *or to learn more about chemical process industries and technical operators, contact*
American Chemical Society
Career Education
1155 16th Street, NW
Washington, DC 20036-4801
Tel: 800-227-5558
Email: help@acs.org
http://www.chemistry.org

The American Chemistry Council offers a great deal of information about the chemical industry and maintains an informative Web site.
American Chemistry Council
1300 Wilson Boulevard
Arlington VA 22209-2323
Tel: 703-741-5000
http://www.americanchemistry.com

For information on chemical engineering, contact
American Institute of Chemical Engineers
3 Park Avenue
New York, NY 10016-5991
Tel: 800-242-4363
http://www.aiche.org

Industrial Designers

OVERVIEW

Industrial designers combine technical knowledge of materials, machines, and production with artistic talent to improve the appearance and function of machine-made products. There are approximately 49,000 industrial designers employed in the United States.

HISTORY

Although industrial design as a separate and unique profession did not develop in the United States until the 1920s, it has its origins in colonial America and the industrial revolution. When colonists were faced with having to make their own products rather than relying on imported goods, they learned to modify existing objects and create new ones. As the advent of the industrial revolution drew near, interest in machinery and industry increased.

One of the earliest examples of industrial design is found in Eli Whitney's production of muskets. In 1800, he promised to manufacture several thousand muskets for the government using the principles of standardization and interchangeable parts. Designs and manufacturing processes for each musket part had to be created. This early example of industrial design involved not only designing an individual product but also the manufacturing processes and the production equipment.

The industrial revolution brought about the mass production of objects and increased machine manufacturing. As production capabilities grew, a group of entrepreneurs, inventors, and designers emerged. Together, these individuals determined products that could be mass-produced and figured out ways to manufacture them.

QUICK FACTS

School Subjects
Art
Mathematics

Personal Skills
Artistic
Technical/scientific

Work Environment
Primarily indoors
Primarily one location

Minimum Education Level
Bachelor's degree

Salary Range
$31,510 to $54,560 to
$125,000

Certification or Licensing
None available

Outlook
About as fast as the average

DOT
142

GOE
01.04.02

NOC
2252

O*NET-SOC
27-1021.00

In the early 1900s, the number of products available to the public grew, as did the purchasing power of individuals. Manufacturers realized that in order to compete with imported goods and skilled craftspersons, they needed to offer a wide variety of products that were well designed and affordable. At that time, manufactured products were designed to be functional, utilitarian, and easily produced by machines. Little attention was paid to aesthetics. Product designs were copied from imported items, and there was little original design.

Consumers were growing increasingly dissatisfied with the products they were offered. They felt that machine-made goods were, in many cases, ugly and unattractive. Manufacturers did not initially respond to these complaints. For example, Henry Ford continued to manufacture only one style of car, the Model T, despite criticism that it looked like a tin can. Ford was unconcerned because he sold more cars than anyone else. When General Motors started selling its attractive Chevrolet in 1926, and it outsold the Ford, he finally recognized the importance of styling and design.

Advertising convincingly demonstrated the importance of design. Those products with artistic features sold better, and manufacturers realized that design did play an important role both in marketing and manufacturing. By 1927, manufacturers were hiring people solely to advise them on design features. Industrial design came to represent a new profession: The practice of using aesthetic design features to create manufactured goods that were economical, served a specific purpose, and satisfied the psychological needs of consumers. Most of the early industrial designers came from Europe until design schools were established in America.

Industrial design as a profession grew rapidly in the years from 1927 until World War II. Many of the early industrial designers established their own firms rather than working directly for a manufacturer. After the war, consumer goods proliferated, which helped the field continue to grow. Manufacturers paid more attention to style and design in an effort to make their products stand out in the marketplace. They began to hire in-house designers. Today, industrial designers play a significant role in both designing new products and determining which products may be successful in the marketplace.

THE JOB

Industrial designers are an integral part of the manufacturing process. They work on creating designs for new products and redesigning existing products. Before a product can be manufactured, a design must be created that specifies its form, function, and appearance. Industrial designers must pay attention to the purpose of the proposed product, anticipated use by consumers, economic factors affecting its design and manufacture, and material and safety requirements.

Industrial designers are usually part of a team that includes engineers, marketing specialists, production personnel, sales representatives, and sometimes, top manufacturing managers. Before the design process actually begins, market research or surveys may be conducted that analyze how well a product is performing, what its market share is, and how well competitors' products are doing. Also, feasibility studies may be conducted to determine whether an existing design should be changed or a new product created to keep or gain market share.

Once a determination is made to create a new design, an industrial designer is assigned to the project. The designer reviews study results and meets with other design team members to develop a concept. The designer studies the features of the proposed product as well as the material requirements and manufacturing costs and requirements. Several designs are sketched and other team members are consulted.

Some designers still create sketches by hand, but most use design software that allows them to create sketches on a computer. Once a preliminary design is selected, designers work out all of the details. They calculate all of the measurements of each part of the design, identify specific components, select necessary materials, and choose colors and other visual elements. A detailed design is then submitted to engineers and other design team members for review.

In some cases, a model or prototype may be built; however, computer-aided design programs now allow engineers to test design features before this stage. Engineers test for performance, strength, durability, and other factors to ensure that a product actually performs as planned and meets all safety and industrial standards. If any part of a product fails to meet test standards, the design is sent back to the industrial designer for revisions.

This process continues until the design passes all test stages. At this point, a model may be built of clay, foam, wood, or other materials to serve as a guide for production. In some cases, a prototype made of the actual materials and components will be built. The design, along with all computer data and any models and prototypes, is turned over to the production department, which is then responsible for manufacturing it.

Industrial designers may also become involved in the marketing and advertising promotion of products. They may name the new product, design the product's packaging, plan promotional campaigns or advertising strategies, and create artwork used for advertising.

Industrial designers may design the layout of franchised businesses, such as clothing stores or gas stations, so that they present a coordinated company image. This type of design can also include developing company symbols, trademarks, and logos.

Designers may work for a design firm or directly for a manufacturing company. They may freelance or set up their own consulting firms. Corporate designers may be part of a large team with designers at various locations. Computer networking allows several designers to work simultaneously on the same project. Using this approach, a designer creates one part of a design, for example, the electronic components, while another designer creates another part, such as the mechanical housing. A variation on the multidesigner approach schedules designers on different shifts to work on the same project.

Technology is changing the way industrial designers work. Computer-aided industrial design tools are revolutionizing the way

Books to Read

Ashby, Michael, and Kara Johnson. *Materials and Design: The Art and Science of Material Selection in Product Design.* Oxford, U.K.: Butterworth-Heinemann, 2002.

Association of Women Industrial Designers. *Goddess in the Details: Product Design by Women.* New York: Association of Women Industrial Designers, 2006.

Fiell, Charlotte. *Industrial Design A-Z.* Los Angeles: Taschen Books, 2006.

Gorman, Carma, ed. *The Industrial Design Reader.* New York: Allworth Press, 2003.

Industrial Designers Society of America. *Design Secrets: Products: 50 Real-Life Product Design Projects.* Gloucester, Mass.: Rockport Publishers, 2001.

Kirkham, Pat, ed. *Women Designers in the USA, 1900-2000: Diversity and Divergence.* New Haven, Conn.: Yale University Press, 2000.

Petroski, Henry. *The Evolution of Useful Things.* New York: Vintage Books, 1994.

Williams, Pamela. *How to Break Into Product Design.* Cincinnati, Ohio: North Light Books, 1998.

products are designed and manufactured. These programs allow designers and engineers to test products during the design stage so that design flaws are identified before prototypes are built. Other programs allow product models to be tested online. Designs can be sent directly to machine tools that produce three-dimensional models. All of these advances decrease the time necessary to design a product, test it, and manufacture it.

REQUIREMENTS

High School

In high school, take as many art and computer classes as possible in addition to college preparatory classes in English, social studies, algebra, geometry, and science. Classes in mechanical drawing may be helpful, but drafting skills are being replaced by the ability to use computers to create graphics and manipulate objects. Science classes, such as physics and chemistry, are also becoming more important as industrial designers select materials and components for products and need to have a basic understanding of scientific principles. Shop classes, such as machine shop, metalworking, and woodworking, are also useful and provide training in using hand and machine tools.

Postsecondary Training

A bachelor's degree in fine arts or industrial design is recommended, although some employers accept diplomas from art schools. Training is offered through art schools, art departments of colleges and universities, and technical colleges. Most bachelor's degree programs require four or five years to complete. Some schools also offer a master's degree, which requires two years of additional study. Often, art schools grant a diploma for three years of study in industrial design. Programs in industrial design are offered by approximately 45 schools accredited (or that are in the process of accreditation) by the National Association of Schools of Art and Design.

School programs vary; some emphasize engineering and technical work, while others emphasize art background. Certain basic courses are common to every school: two-dimensional design (color theory, spatial organization) and three-dimensional design (abstract sculpture, art structures). Students also have a great deal of studio practice; learning to make models of clay, plaster, wood, and other easily worked materials. Some schools even use metalworking machinery. Technically oriented schools generally require a course in basic engineering. Schools offering degree programs also require courses in English, history, science, and other basic subjects. Such courses as merchandising and business are important for anyone working in a field so closely connected with the consumer. Most schools also offer classes in computer-aided design and computer graphics. One of the most essential skills for success as an industrial designer is the ability to use design software.

Other Requirements

Industrial designers are creative, have artistic ability, and are able to work closely with others in a collaborative style. In general, designers do not crave fame or recognition because designing is a joint project involving the skills of many people. In most cases, industrial designers remain anonymous and behind the scenes. Successful designers can accept criticism and differences of opinion and be open to new ideas.

EXPLORING

An excellent way to uncover an aptitude for design and to gain practical experience in using computers is to take a computer graphics course through an art school, high school continuing education program, technical school, or community college. Some community colleges allow high school students to enroll in classes if no comparable course is offered at the high school level. If no formal training is available, teach yourself how to use a popular graphics software package.

Summer or part-time employment in an industrial design office is a good way to learn more about the profession and what industrial designers do. Another option is to work in an advertising agency or for a market research firm. Although these companies most likely won't have an industrial designer on staff, they will provide exposure to how to study consumer trends and plan marketing promotions.

Pursue hobbies such as sculpting, ceramics, jewelry making, woodworking, and sketching to develop creative and artistic abilities. Reading about industrial design can also be very beneficial. Publications such as *Design News* (http://www.designnews.com) contain many interesting and informative articles that describe different design products and report on current trends. This magazine can be found at many public libraries. Read books on the history of industrial design to learn about interesting case studies on the development of specific products.

EMPLOYERS

Approximately 49,000 industrial designers are employed in the United States. Industrial designers work in all areas of industry. Some specialize in consumer products, such as household appliances, home entertainment items, personal computers, clothing, jewelry, and car stereos. Others work in designing automobiles, electronic devices, airplanes, biomedical products, medical equipment, measuring instruments, or office equipment. Most designers specialize in a specific area of manufacturing and work on only a few types of products.

STARTING OUT

Most employers prefer to hire someone who has a degree or diploma from a college, art school, or technical school. Persons with engineering, architectural, or other scientific backgrounds also have a good chance at entry-level jobs, especially if they have artistic and creative talent. When interviewing for a job, a designer should be prepared to present a portfolio of work.

Job openings may be listed through a college career services office or in classified ads in newspapers or trade magazines. Qualified beginners may also apply directly to companies that hire industrial designers. Several directories listing industrial design firms can be found in most public libraries. In addition, lists of industrial design firms appear periodically in magazines such as *BusinessWeek* and *Engineering News-Record*. Also, a new industrial designer can get a free copy of *Getting An Industrial Design Job* at the Web site of the Industrial Designers Society of America (http://www.idsa.org).

ADVANCEMENT

Entry-level industrial designers usually begin as assistants to other designers. They do routine work and hold little responsibility for design changes. With experience and the necessary qualifications, the designer may be promoted to a higher-ranking position with major responsibility for design. Experienced designers may be promoted to project managers or move into supervisory positions. Supervisory positions may include overseeing and coordinating the work of several designers, including freelancers and industrial designers at outside agencies. Some senior designers are given a free hand in designing products. With experience, established reputation, and financial backing, some industrial designers decide to open their own consulting firms.

EARNINGS

According to the Industrial Designers Society of America, the average starting salary for industrial designers is $36,000. Designers with five years' experience earn an average of $58,000 a year. Senior designers with 10 years' experience earn $73,000. Industrial designers with 19 years or more of experience earn average salaries of $125,000. Managers who direct design departments in large companies earn substantially more. Owners or partners of consulting firms have fluctuating incomes, depending on their business for the year.

According to the U.S. Department of Labor, industrial designers earned a median annual salary of $54,560 in 2006. The lowest 10 percent earned less than $31,510 annually, and the top 10 percent earned more than $92,970.

WORK ENVIRONMENT

Industrial designers enjoy generally pleasant work conditions. In many companies, the atmosphere is relaxed and casual. Most designers spend a significant amount of time at either a computer workstation or drawing board. Most industrial designers work at least 40 hours a week, with overtime frequently required. There is a lot of pressure to speed up the design/development process and get products to market as soon as possible. For some designers, this can mean regularly working 10 to 20 hours or more of overtime a week. Working on weekends and into the evening can be required to run a special computer program or to work on a project with a tight deadline. Designers who freelance, or work for themselves, set their own hours but may work more than 40 hours a week in order to meet the needs of their clients.

OUTLOOK

Employment of industrial designers is expected to grow about as fast as the average for all occupations through 2014, according to the U.S. Department of Labor (DOL). This favorable outlook is based on the need to improve product quality and safety, to design new products for the global marketplace, and to design high-tech products in consumer electronics, medicine, and transportation. The DOL predicts that designers who combine business expertise with an educational background in engineering and computer-aided design will have the best employment prospects.

Despite the demand for industrial designers, many companies prefer to outsource a significant amount of their work. This is a growing trend within the industry that may make it more difficult for a beginning worker to find an entry-level job. In addition, this is a profession that is somewhat controlled by the economic climate. It thrives in times of prosperity and declines in periods of recession.

FOR MORE INFORMATION

*For information on opportunities for women in industrial design,
contact*
Association of Women Industrial Designers
Old Chelsea Station
PO Box 468
New York, NY 10011
Email: info@awidweb.com
http://www.awidweb.com

*For information on careers, educational programs, and a free copy
of* Getting an Industrial Design Job, *contact*
Industrial Designers Society of America
45195 Business Court, Suite 250
Dulles, VA 20166-6717
Tel: 703-707-6000
Email: idsa@idsa.org
http://www.idsa.org

For information on accredited design schools, contact
National Association of Schools of Art and Design
11250 Roger Bacon Drive, Suite 21
Reston, VA 20190-5248
Tel: 703-437-0700
Email: info@arts-accredit.org
http://nasad.arts-accredit.org

Industrial Engineers

OVERVIEW

Industrial engineers use their knowledge of various disciplines—including systems engineering, management science, operations research, and fields such as ergonomics—to determine the most efficient and cost-effective methods for industrial production. They are responsible for designing systems that integrate materials, equipment, information, and people in the overall production process. Approximately 177,000 industrial engineers are employed in the United States.

HISTORY

In today's industries, manufacturers increasingly depend on industrial engineers to determine the most efficient production techniques and processes. The roots of industrial engineering, however, can be traced to ancient Greece, where records indicate that manufacturing labor was divided among people having specialized skills.

The most significant milestones in industrial engineering, before the field even had an official name, occurred in the 18th century, when a number of inventions were introduced in the textile industry. The first was the flying shuttle that opened the door to the highly automatic weaving we now take for granted. This shuttle allowed one person, rather than two, to weave fabrics wider than ever before. Other innovative devices, such as the power loom and the spinning jenny that increased weaving speed and improved quality, soon followed. By the late 18th century, the industrial revolution was in full swing. Innovations in manufacturing were made, standardization of interchangeable parts was implemented, and specialization of labor was increasingly put into practice.

QUICK FACTS

School Subjects
Computer science
Mathematics

Personal Skills
Leadership/management
Technical/scientific

Work Environment
Primarily indoors
Primarily one location

Minimum Education Level
Bachelor's degree

Salary Range
$44,790 to $68,620 to $100,980+

Certification or Licensing
Required by certain states

Outlook
About as fast as the average

DOT
012

GOE
02.07.02

NOC
2141

O*NET-SOC
17-2112.00

Industrial engineering as a science is said to have originated with the work of Frederick Taylor. In 1881, he began to study the way production workers used their time. At the Midvale Steel Company where he was employed, he introduced the concept of time study, whereby workers were timed with a stopwatch and their production was evaluated. He used the studies to design methods and equipment that allowed tasks to be done more efficiently.

In the early 1900s, the field was known as scientific management. Frank and Lillian Gilbreth were influential with their motion studies of workers performing various tasks. Then, around 1913, automaker Henry Ford implemented a conveyor belt assembly line in his factory, which led to increasingly integrated production lines in more and more companies. Industrial engineers nowadays are called upon to solve ever more complex operating problems and to design systems involving large numbers of workers, complicated equipment, and vast amounts of information. They meet this challenge by utilizing advanced computers and software to design complex mathematical models and other simulations.

THE JOB

Industrial engineers are involved with the development and implementation of the systems and procedures that are utilized by many industries and businesses. In general, they figure out the most effective ways to use the three basic elements of any company: people, facilities, and equipment.

Although industrial engineers work in a variety of businesses, the main focus of the discipline is in manufacturing, also called industrial production. Primarily, industrial engineers are concerned with process technology, which includes the design and layout of machinery and the organization of workers who implement the required tasks.

Industrial engineers have many responsibilities. With regard to facilities and equipment, engineers are involved in selecting machinery and other equipment and then in setting them up in the most efficient production layout. They also develop methods to accomplish production tasks, such as the organization of an assembly line. In addition, they devise systems for quality control, distribution, and inventory.

Industrial engineers are also responsible for some organizational issues. For instance, they might study an organization chart and other information about a project and then determine the functions and responsibilities of workers. They devise and implement job evaluation procedures as well as articulate labor-utilization standards for workers. Engineers often meet with managers to discuss cost

Earnings by Specialty, 2006

Industry	Mean Annual Earnings
ISPs and Web search portals	$85,600
Magnetic media manufacturing and reproducing	$85,160
Oil and gas extraction	$84,410
Specialized design services	$80,860
Electronic instrument manufacturing	$76,430
Semiconductor and electronic component manufacturing	$76,260
Commercial equipment merchant wholesalers	$74,970
Architectural and engineering services	$74,310
Aerospace product and parts manufacturing	$71,100
Motor vehicle parts manufacturing	$67,300

Source: U.S. Department of Labor

analysis, financial planning, job evaluation, and salary administration. Not only do they recommend methods for improving employee efficiency, but they may also devise wage and incentive programs.

Industrial engineers also evaluate ergonomic issues—the relationship between human capabilities and the physical environment in which they work. For example, they might evaluate whether machines are causing physical harm or discomfort to workers or whether the machines could be designed differently to enable workers to be more productive.

REQUIREMENTS

High School

To prepare for a college engineering program, concentrate on mathematics (algebra, trigonometry, geometry, calculus), physical sciences (physics, chemistry), social sciences (economics, sociology), and English. Engineers often have to convey ideas graphically and may need to visualize processes in three dimensions, so courses in graphics, drafting, or design are also helpful. In addition, round out your education with computer science, history, and foreign language classes. If honor-level courses are available to you, be sure to take them.

Postsecondary Training

A bachelor's degree from an accredited institution is usually the minimum requirement for all professional positions. The Accreditation Board for Engineering and Technology (ABET) accredits schools offering engineering programs, including industrial engineering. A listing of accredited colleges and universities is available on the ABET Web site (http://www.abet.org), and a visit here should be one of your first stops when you are deciding on a school to attend. Colleges and universities offer either four- or five-year engineering programs. Because of the intensity of the curricula, many students take heavy course loads and attend summer sessions in order to finish in four years.

During your junior and senior years of college, you should consider your specific career goals, such as in which industry to work. Third- and fourth-year courses focus on such subjects as facility planning and design, work measurement standards, process design, engineering economics, manufacturing and automation, and incentive plans.

Many industrial engineers go on to earn a graduate degree. These programs tend to involve more research and independent study. Graduate degrees are usually required for teaching positions.

Certification or Licensing

Licensure as a professional engineer is recommended since an increasing number of employers require it. Even those employers who do not require licensing will view it favorably when considering new hires or when reviewing workers for promotion. Licensing requirements vary from state to state. In general, however, they involve having graduated from an accredited school, having four years of work experience, and having passed the eight-hour Fundamentals of Engineering exam and the eight-hour Principles and Practice of Engineering exam. Depending on your state of residence, you can take the Fundamentals exam shortly before your graduation from college or after you have received your bachelor's degree. At that point you will be an engineer-in-training. Once you have fulfilled all the licensure requirements, you receive the designation professional engineer.

Other Requirements

Industrial engineers enjoy problem solving and analyzing things as well as being a team member. The ability to communicate is vital since engineers interact with all levels of management and workers. Being organized and detail-minded is important because industrial engineers often handle large projects and must bring them in on time and on budget. Since process design is the cornerstone of the field, an engineer should be creative and inventive.

EXPLORING

Try joining a science or engineering club, such as the Junior Engineering Technical Society (JETS). JETS offers academic competitions in subjects such as computer fundamentals, mathematics, physics, and English. It also conducts design contests in which students learn and apply science and engineering principles. JETS also offers the *Pre-Engineering Times*, a publication that will be useful if you are interested in engineering. It contains information on engineering specialties, competitions, schools, scholarships, and other resources. Visit http://www.jets.org/publications/petimes.cfm to read the publication. You also might read some engineering books for background on the field or magazines such as *Industrial Engineer*, a magazine published by the Institute of Industrial Engineers (IIE). Selected articles from *Industrial Engineer* can be viewed on the IIE's Web site, http://www.iienet.org.

EMPLOYERS

Approximately 177,000 industrial engineers are employed in the United States. Although a majority of industrial engineers are employed in the manufacturing industry, related jobs are found in almost all businesses, including aviation; aerospace; transportation; communications; electric, gas, and sanitary services; government; finance; insurance; real estate; wholesale and retail trade; construction; mining; agriculture; forestry; and fishing. Also, many work as independent consultants.

STARTING OUT

The main qualification for an entry-level job is a bachelor's degree in industrial engineering. Accredited college programs generally have job openings listed in their career services offices. Entry-level industrial engineers find jobs in various departments, such as computer operations, warehousing, and quality control. As engineers gain on-the-job experience and familiarity with departments, they may decide on a specialty. Some may want to continue to work as process designers or methods engineers, while others may move on to administrative positions.

Some further examples of specialties include work measurement standards, shipping and receiving, cost control, engineering economics, materials handling, management information systems, mathematical models, and operations. Many who choose industrial engineering as a career find its appeal in the diversity of sectors that are available to explore.

ADVANCEMENT

After having worked at least three years in the same job, an industrial engineer may have the basic credentials needed for advancement to a higher position. In general, positions in operations and administration are considered high-level jobs, although this varies from company to company. Engineers who work in these areas tend to earn larger salaries than those who work in warehousing or cost control, for example. If one is interested in moving to a different company, it is considered easier to do so within the same industry.

Industrial engineering jobs are often considered stepping-stones to management positions, even in other fields. Engineers with many years' experience frequently are promoted to higher level jobs with greater responsibilities. Because of the field's broad exposure, industrial engineering employees are generally considered better prepared for executive roles than are other types of engineers.

EARNINGS

According to the U.S. Department of Labor, the median annual wage for industrial engineers in 2006 was $68,620. The lowest paid 10 percent of all industrial engineers earned less than $44,790 annually. However, as with most occupations, salaries rise as more experience is gained. Very experienced engineers can earn more than $100,980. According to a survey by the National Association of Colleges and Employers, the average starting salary for industrial engineers with a bachelor's degree was $49,567 in 2005, while those with a master's degree earned $56,561 a year; and those with a Ph.D. earned $85,000.

WORK ENVIRONMENT

Industrial engineers usually work in offices at desks and computers, designing and evaluating plans, statistics, and other documents. Overall, industrial engineering is ranked above other engineering disciplines for factors such as employment outlook, salary, and physical environment. However, industrial engineering jobs are considered stressful because they often entail tight deadlines and demanding quotas, and jobs are moderately competitive. Engineers work an average of 46 hours per week.

Industrial engineers generally collaborate with other employees, conferring on designs and procedures, as well as with business managers and consultants. Although they spend most of their time in their offices, they frequently must evaluate conditions at factories and plants, where noise levels are often high.

OUTLOOK

The U.S. Department of Labor anticipates that employment for industrial engineers will grow about as fast as the average for all occupations through 2014. The demand for industrial engineers will continue as manufacturing and other companies strive to make their production processes more effective and competitive. Engineers who transfer or retire will create the highest percentage of openings in this field.

FOR MORE INFORMATION

For a list of ABET-accredited engineering schools, contact
Accreditation Board for Engineering and Technology (ABET)
111 Market Place, Suite 1050
Baltimore, MD 21202-7116
Tel: 410-347-7700
http://www.abet.org

For comprehensive information about careers in industrial engineering, contact
Institute of Industrial Engineers
3577 Parkway Lane, Suite 200
Norcross, GA 30092-2833
Tel: 800-494-0460
http://www.iienet.org

Visit the JETS Web site for membership information and to read the online brochure Industrial Engineering.
Junior Engineering Technical Society (JETS)
1420 King Street, Suite 405
Alexandria, VA 22314-2794
Tel: 703-548-5387
Email: info@jets.org
http://www.jets.org

Industrial Machinery Mechanics

OVERVIEW

Industrial machinery mechanics, often called *machinery maintenance mechanics* or *industrial machinery repairers,* inspect, maintain, repair, and adjust industrial production and processing machinery and equipment to ensure its proper operation in various industries. There are approximately 220,000 industrial machinery mechanics employed in the United States.

HISTORY

Before 1750 and the beginning of the industrial revolution in Europe, almost all work was done by hand. Families grew their own food, wove their own cloth, and bought or traded very little. Gradually the economic landscape changed. Factories mass-produced products that had once been created by hand. The spinning jenny, a multiple-spindle machine for spinning wool or cotton, was one of the first machines of the industrial revolution. After it came a long procession of inventions and developments, including the steam engine, power loom, cotton gin, steamboat, locomotive, telegraph, and Bessemer converter. With these machines came the need for people who could maintain and repair them.

Mechanics learned that all machines are based on six configurations: the lever, the wheel and axle, the pulley, the inclined plane, the wedge, and the screw. By combining these elements in more complex ways, the machines could do more work in less time than people or animals could do. Thus, the role of machinery mechanics

QUICK FACTS

School Subjects
Mathematics
Technical/shop

Personal Skills
Mechanical/manipulative
Technical/scientific

Work Environment
Primarily indoors
Primarily one location

Minimum Education Level
Apprenticeship

Salary Range
$26,710 to $41,050 to
$62,080+

Certification or Licensing
None available

Outlook
More slowly than the average

DOT
626

GOE
05.03.02

NOC
7311

O*NET-SOC
49-9041.00, 49-9041.43

became vital in keeping production lines running and businesses profitable.

The industrial revolution continues even today, although now it is known as the age of automation. As machines become more numerous and more complex, the work of the industrial machinery mechanic becomes even more necessary.

THE JOB

The types of machinery on which industrial machinery mechanics work are as varied as the types of industries operating in the United States today. Mechanics are employed in metal stamping plants, printing plants, chemical and plastics plants, and almost any type of large-scale industrial operation that can be imagined. The machinery in these plants must be maintained regularly. Breakdowns and delays with one machine can hinder a plant's entire operation, which is costly for the company.

Preventive maintenance is a major part of mechanics' jobs. They inspect the equipment, oil and grease moving components, and clean and repair parts. They also keep detailed maintenance records on the equipment they service. They often follow blueprints and engineering specifications to maintain and fix equipment.

When breakdowns occur, mechanics may partially or completely disassemble a machine to make the necessary repairs. They replace worn bearings, adjust clutches, and replace and repair defective parts. They may have to order replacement parts from the machinery's manufacturer. If no parts are available, they may have to make the necessary replacements, using milling machines, lathes, or other tooling equipment. After the machine is reassembled, they may have to make adjustments to its operational settings. They often work with the machine's regular operator to test it. When repairing electronically controlled machinery, mechanics may work closely with electronic repairers or electricians who maintain the machine's electronic parts.

Often these mechanics can identify potential breakdowns and fix problems before any real damage or delays occur. They may notice that a machine is vibrating, rattling, or squeaking, or they may see that the items produced by the machine are flawed. Many types of new machinery are built with programmed internal evaluation systems that check the accuracy and condition of equipment. This assists mechanics in their jobs, but it also makes them responsible for maintaining the check-up systems.

Machinery installations are becoming another facet of a mechanic's job. As plants retool and invest in new equipment, they rely on

An industrial machinery mechanic services a turbine. *(Corbis)*

mechanics to properly situate and install the machinery. In many plants, millwrights traditionally did this job, but as employers increasingly seek workers with multiple skills, industrial machinery mechanics are taking on new responsibilities.

Industrial machinery mechanics use a wide range of tools when doing preventive maintenance or making repairs. For example, they may use simple tools such as a screwdriver and wrench to repair an engine or a hoist to lift a printing press off the ground. Sometimes they solder or weld equipment. They use power and hand tools and precision measuring instruments. In some shops, mechanics troubleshoot the entire plant's operations. Others may become experts in electronics, hydraulics, pneumatics, or other specialties.

REQUIREMENTS

High School

While most employers prefer to hire those who have completed high school, opportunities do exist for those without a diploma as long as they have had some kind of related training. While you are in high school, take courses in mechanical drawing, general mathematics, algebra, and geometry. Other classes that will help prepare you for this career are physics, computer science, and electronics. Any class that gives you experience in blueprint reading adds to your qualifications.

Postsecondary Training

In the past, most industrial machinery mechanics learned the skills of the trade informally by spending several years as helpers in a particular factory. Currently, as machinery has become more complex, more formal training is necessary. Today many mechanics learn the trade through apprenticeship programs sponsored by a local trade union. Apprenticeship programs usually last four years and include both on-the-job and related classroom training. In addition to the use and care of machine and hand tools, apprentices learn the operation, lubrication, and adjustment of the machinery and equipment they will maintain. In class they learn shop mathematics, blueprint reading, safety, hydraulics, welding, and other subjects related to the trade.

Students may also obtain training through vocational or technical schools. Useful programs are those that offer machine shop courses and provide training in electronics and numerical control machine tools.

Other Requirements

Students interested in this field should possess mechanical aptitude and manual dexterity. Good physical condition and agility are necessary because as a mechanic you will sometimes have to lift heavy objects, crawl under large machines, or climb to reach equipment located high above the factory floor.

Mechanics are responsible for valuable equipment and are often called upon to exercise considerable independent judgment. Because of technological advances, you should be willing to learn the requirements of new machines and production techniques. When a plant purchases new equipment, the equipment's manufacturer often trains plant employees in proper operation and maintenance. Technological change requires mechanics to be adaptable and to have inquiring minds.

EXPLORING

If you are interested in this field, you should take as many shop courses as you can. Exploring and repairing machinery, such as automobiles and home appliances, will also sharpen your skills. In addition, try landing part-time work or a summer job in an industrial plant that gives you the opportunity to observe industrial repair work being done.

EMPLOYERS

Approximately 220,000 industrial machinery mechanics are employed in the United States. These mechanics work in a wide variety of plants and are employed in every part of the country, although employment is concentrated in industrialized areas. According to the U.S. Department of Labor, two-thirds of all industrial machinery mechanics work in manufacturing industries such as chemicals, motor vehicles, food processing, textile mill products, primary metals, and fabricated metal products. Others work for public utilities, government agencies, and mining companies.

STARTING OUT

Jobs can be obtained by directly applying to companies that use industrial equipment or machinery. The majority of mechanics work for manufacturing plants. These plants are found in a wide variety of industries, including the automotive, plastics, textile, electronics, packaging, food, beverage, and aerospace industries. Chances for job openings may be better at a large plant. New workers are generally assigned to work as helpers or trainees.

Prospective mechanics may also learn of job openings or apprenticeship programs through local unions. Industrial mechanics may be represented by one of several unions, depending on their industry and place of employment. These unions include the International Union, United Automobile, Aerospace, and Agricultural Implement Workers of America; the United Steelworkers of America; the United Auto Workers; the International Union of Electronic, Electrical, Salaried, Machine, and Furniture Workers–Communications Workers of America; the United Brotherhood of Carpenters and Joiners of America; and the International Association of Machinists and Aerospace Workers. According to the U.S. Department of Labor, approximately 25 percent of all industrial machinery mechanics are members of a union. Private and state employment offices are other good sources of job openings.

ADVANCEMENT

Those who begin as helpers or trainees usually become journeymen in four years. Although opportunities for advancement beyond this rank are somewhat limited, industrial machinery mechanics who learn more complicated machinery and equipment can advance into higher-paying positions. The most highly skilled mechanics may be promoted to master mechanics. Those who demonstrate good leadership and interpersonal skills can become supervisors. Skilled mechanics also have the option of becoming machinists, numerical control tool programmers, precision metalworkers, packaging machinery technicians, and robotics technicians. Some of these positions do require additional training, but the skills of a mechanic readily transfer to these areas.

EARNINGS

In 2006, median hourly earnings for industrial machinery mechanics were $19.74 (or $41,050 annually), according to the U.S. Department of Labor. The lowest paid 10 percent earned less than $12.84 an hour (or $26,710 annually). The highest 10 percent earned $29.85 or more per hour (or $62,080 annually). Apprentices generally earn lower wages and earn incremental raises as they advance in their training. Earnings vary based on experience, skills, type of industry, and geographic location. Those working in union plants generally earn more than those in nonunion plants. Most industrial machinery mechanics are provided with benefit packages, which can include paid holidays and vacations; medical, dental, and life insurance; and retirement plans.

WORK ENVIRONMENT

Industrial machinery mechanics work in all types of manufacturing plants, which may be hot, noisy, and dirty or relatively quiet and clean. Mechanics frequently work with greasy, dirty equipment and need to be able to adapt to a variety of physical conditions. Because machinery is not always accessible, mechanics may have to work in stooped or cramped positions or on high ladders.

Although working around machinery poses some danger, this risk is minimized with proper safety precautions. Modern machinery includes many safety features and devices, and most plants follow good safety practices. Mechanics often wear protective clothing and equipment, such as hard hats and safety belts, glasses, and shoes.

Mechanics work with little supervision and need to be able to work well with others. They need to be flexible and respond to changing priorities, which can result in interruptions that pull a mechanic off one job to repair a more urgent problem. Although the standard workweek is 40 hours, overtime is common. Because factories and other sites cannot afford breakdowns, industrial machinery mechanics may be called to the plant at night or on weekends for emergency repairs.

OUTLOOK

The U.S. Department of Labor predicts that employment for industrial machinery mechanics will grow more slowly than the average for all occupations through 2014. Some industries will have a greater need for mechanics than others. Much of the new automated production equipment that companies are purchasing has its own self-diagnostic capabilities and is more reliable than older equipment. Although this machinery still needs to be maintained, most job openings will stem from the replacement of transferring or retiring workers.

Certain industries are extremely susceptible to changing economic factors and reduce production activities in slow periods. During these periods, companies may lay off workers or reduce hours. Mechanics are less likely to be laid off than other workers as machines need to be maintained regardless of production levels. Slower production periods and temporary shutdowns are often used to overhaul equipment. Nonetheless, employment opportunities are generally better at companies experiencing growth or stable levels of production.

Because machinery is becoming more complex and automated, mechanics need to be more highly skilled than in the past. Mechanics who stay up to date with new technologies, particularly those related to electronics and computers, should find favorable employment opportunities over the next decade.

FOR MORE INFORMATION

For information about apprentice programs, contact the UAW.
International Union, United Automobile, Aerospace, and
    Agricultural Implement Workers of America (UAW)
8000 East Jefferson Avenue
Detroit, MI 48214-3963
Tel: 313-926-5000
http://www.uaw.org

For information about the machining industry and career opportunities, contact
National Tooling and Machining Association
9300 Livingston Road
Fort Washington, MD 20744-4914

Tel: 800-248-6862
http://www.ntma.org

For industry information, contact
Precision Machined Products Association
6700 West Snowville Road
Brecksville, OH 44141-3212
Tel: 440-526-0300
http://www.pmpa.org

Industrial Safety and Health Technicians

OVERVIEW

Industrial safety and health technicians are part of a management team of an industrial plant. Their job is to make the workplace as safe as possible. Industrial safety and health technicians take direction from plant managers, industrial engineers, and government agencies to verify that machinery and the physical plant meet established safety codes. They make sure that workers understand required safety procedures, and they also work to ensure workers' compliance with these important safety measures.

HISTORY

In the 18th century, when the industrial revolution began, waterpower and steam-driven machines made mass production possible. The primary objective then was to achieve high production rates. Safety on the job was often considered the responsibility of the worker, not the employer.

By the beginning of the 20th century, working conditions had vastly improved. Workers and employers found that the cost of injuries and the loss of production and wages from industrial accidents were very expensive to both parties. Industry owners and labor leaders began to use safety engineering methods to prevent industrial accidents and diseases.

The combined efforts of business, government, and labor organizations resulted in increased safety awareness and much safer and healthier working environments. Industrial safety engineers and

QUICK FACTS

School Subjects
Health
Technical/shop

Personal Skills
Helping/teaching
Leadership/management

Work Environment
Primarily indoors
Primarily one location

Minimum Education Level
Associate's degree

Salary Range
$25,240 to $42,160 to
$100,000+

Certification or Licensing
Voluntary

Outlook
About as fast as the average

DOT
168

GOE
04.04.02

NOC
2263

O*NET-SOC
17-2111.01, 29-9011.00,
29-9012.00

industrial hygienists studied accidents and learned how to make workplaces safer for employees, leading to the development of industrial safety standards and practices.

With the passage of the Occupational Safety and Health Act (OSHA) in 1970, highly developed and accepted standards for safety and health in the workplace became the legal responsibility of employers. Many large industrial companies with established safety programs hired safety and health technicians to make sure that their operations met OSHA requirements. Failure to meet OSHA requirements would result in fines.

After this legislation, companies large and small that had no formal safety programs hired safety professionals and enacted programs to ensure OSHA compliance. Insurance companies expanded their loss-control consulting staffs, and the number of independent safety consulting firms increased because many small businesses needed informed and reliable help to make their workplaces safe under the law.

The demand for trained safety and health personnel increased accordingly. Today, continued public support and concern for occupational safety and health has made it clear that there is a need for broadly educated, specially trained, and highly skilled industrial safety and health technicians.

THE JOB

There were 4.2 million cases of nonfatal work-related sickness or injury in the United States in 2005, according to the Bureau of Labor Statistics. About 1.2 million of these cases were serious enough to cause at least one lost workday. Many cases involve far more time lost from work and sometimes even death. In 2005, 5,702 fatal work injuries occurred. It is the task of the industrial safety and health staff, including technicians, to prevent on-the-job accidents and illnesses.

Industrial safety and health technicians work for many kinds of employers. These include manufacturing industries and businesses, construction and drilling companies, transportation, mining, and other industrial employers, and medical, educational, and scientific institutions. Experienced industrial safety and health technicians may work as instructors with programs for training safety personnel, in federal, state, and local government agencies, insurance firms, and safety consulting firms.

These technicians usually work as members of a team directed by a safety engineer or the head of the engineering department. Many times, the team works relatively independently, following safety plans drawn up by engineers or outside consultants. Depending on their backgrounds, experience, or the nature of the workplace, industrial safety and health technicians may be asked to assume responsibility for safety within a given department, a single site, or several locations.

The work of these technicians is typically a combination of three general activities. The first is to communicate safety consciousness and teach safety practices to employees. Their second duty is to perform on-the-job inspections and analyze potential safety and health hazards in the workplace. Thirdly, technicians write reports, keep records, work with engineers to design safeguards, study ways to improve safety, and communicate suggestions to supervisors.

Safety and health technicians are usually expected to work with the personnel department to organize, schedule, and conduct safety instruction sessions for new workers. Most of the instruction sessions for new employees involve orientation and tours through the areas where they will work. Tours include explanations of the safeguards, safety rules, protection systems, hazards, safety signs, and warnings. They also cover any work rules regarding safety shoes, clothing, glasses, hard hats, and other safety regulations.

These instructional duties are among the technician's most important activities. Understanding and avoiding the actions that cause injury in the first place is more effective than simply reacting to workplace illnesses and accidents after they happen.

Potential hazards in the workplace that are monitored by technicians include airborne health hazards, such as dusts, mists, fumes, and gases; physical hazards, such as noise, vibration, extreme temperatures, and pressure; and mechanical and electrical hazards such as unguarded machinery or improperly grounded or insulated equipment. Technicians also review facilities, checking working surfaces, fire protection systems, sanitation facilities, and electricity and water utilities.

More specialized tasks performed by industrial safety and health technicians cover many areas. They conduct periodic workplace investigations to discover and define substances, conditions, and activities that may contribute to the contamination of a work environment. Technicians review safety evaluation reports from state and insurance inspectors, worker committees, or management to help coordinate actions needed to correct hazards. They also inspect and maintain records on safety equipment, arranging for any necessary repairs.

Technicians may review operating, maintenance, and emergency instructions to be sure that they are adequate and timely. They assist in accident and injury investigations and maintain follow-up records to make sure that corrective actions were taken after an incident.

They recommend to their supervisors ways to improve the company's safety and health performance record and work with management to create a more effective safety policy. This may involve studying current safety reports and attending industrial safety and health conferences.

Technicians also maintain records of the company workers' compensation program and OSHA illness or injury reports. These duties are coordinated with the company's personnel and accounting departments.

In companies with large safety and health staffs, the work of technicians may be more specialized. For example, they may only conduct inspections and design safeguards to prevent accidents. In smaller companies, the beginning technician may be considered the *safety engineer,* responsible for an entire occupational safety program that has been prepared by an outside consultant.

REQUIREMENTS

High School

While in high school, take classes that will prepare you for a two-year industrial safety and health program at a technical or community college. Recommended courses include English with special emphasis on writing and speech, algebra, and science classes with laboratory study. Other valuable courses are computer science, shop, and mechanical drawing.

Postsecondary Training

A two-year program for industrial safety and health technicians involves intensive classroom study with equally intensive laboratory study. In fact, students will typically spend more time in the laboratory than the classroom.

The first year of study usually includes fundamentals of fire protection, safety and health regulations and codes, advanced first aid, and record keeping. The second year typically covers industrial chemical hazards, materials handling and storage, environmental health, sanitation and public health, and disaster preparedness.

If you plan to advance from the position of technician, a four-year degree is recommended. According to the Board of Certified Safety Professionals, more than 90 percent of those in industrial safety positions have earned a bachelor's degree. Though many major in safety, others pursue degrees in engineering, science, or business.

Certification or Licensing

The Occupational Safety and Health Administration and the American Society of Safety Engineers provide safety training programs to corporate employees and to the general public. After course completion, participants receive an official certificate.

The Board of Certified Safety Professionals offers the designation certified safety professional (CSP) to eligible candidates. Though not required, certification has many advantages. For example, a recent salary survey reported that safety professionals with the CSP designation earned 15 to 20 percent more than those who were not certified.

The American Board of Industrial Hygiene also offers the certified industrial hygienist and certified associate industrial hygienist designations. Candidates must have training and education in the field of industrial hygiene, complete an application, and pass a written examination.

Other Requirements

Physical requirements for this career include strong eyesight and adequate physical strength and coordination. Color blindness can be a limiting factor because most factories or industrial plants have color-coded wiring and piping systems. Adequate hearing is needed to interpret normal and abnormal sounds in the workplace that might indicate potential health or safety hazards.

Technicians must be able to make careful, systematic, step-by-step analyses of possible industrial accidents or illness in many different kinds of workplaces. As a result, they should be patient, detail oriented, and thorough in their work. Careful inspections protect the health and lives of hundreds of workers.

EXPLORING

To learn more about the career, talk to a career guidance counselor about your interest in the safety professions. He or she may have advice on how to research the job, visit a plant, or meet with a working industrial safety and health technician. If you live near a community college with a safety and health program, visit its career information center, library, and counseling staff to learn more about the career.

Local OSHA offices and chapters of the National Safety Council can also provide excellent information about this career. Safety publications, such as *Safety+Health* magazine (http://www.nsc.org), also provide information about occupational safety.

Summer or part-time work in manufacturing or warehousing can introduce you to the environments in which you might eventually work. Learning on-the-job safety and health rules in a factory, plant, or other workplace serves as good experience.

EMPLOYERS

According to the Board of Certified Safety Professionals, 32 percent of safety professionals are employed in manufacturing and production industries. Other safety professionals work in the construction, transportation, mining, petroleum, and medical industries. Technicians work for a wide variety of employers, large and small. At a large company, technicians are likely to be part of a large safety and health staff, with their own areas of specialization and responsibilities. At a small company, the safety and health staff may consist of just one or two technicians who assume full responsibility for the entire operation.

Most manufacturing companies have a safety officer, an industrial hygienist, or a safety engineer. In addition, many insurance companies have safety and health specialists on their staffs. Some industrial safety and health technicians work for the government, chiefly for OSHA, or as instructors at community colleges.

STARTING OUT

Many graduates of industrial safety and health technology programs find their first jobs before graduation because recruiters regularly visit schools with such programs. School career services officers identify graduating students that may be interested in jobs in industrial safety so that recruiters can interview and sometimes even make job offers on the spot. Work study arrangements can also result in placements for students after graduation.

Another method of entering a technician career is by first working as an assistant to a safety engineer or a member of the industrial safety and health staff of a large company. After gaining some experience and making contacts in the industry, a more involved job in occupational safety may become available.

Some individuals who join industrial safety and health staffs have trained in specialized work, such as arc welding, machining, foundry work, or metal forming, all of which can be especially hazardous. These experienced workers have already learned safety and health principles while on the job. With additional study, these workers can become industrial safety and health technicians in their specific fields.

ADVANCEMENT

Advancement for industrial safety and health technicians usually results from formal training and continued study. Job experience and exceptional work performance may also lead to a promotion and more responsibility. Keeping abreast of developments and safety practices can help to reduce costs, increase productivity, and improve worker morale and company image. Technicians who help make such improvements in the workplace usually receive higher status and salary with time.

Safety technicians employed by large organizations with specialized departments can work in different areas of the safety system throughout the plant. After working at various assignments, they may advance to a supervisory position overseeing multiple departments or work areas.

After several years of experience and a good record of success, technicians can become specialized safety consultants or government inspectors. Some even become private consultants to insurance companies or small businesses. Many small companies cannot afford a full-time safety engineer and instead hire a consultant to set up an industrial safety and health plan. In such cases, the chief consultant responsible for the newly enacted plan may return periodically to check that all is working and suggest changes where needed. All of these advanced positions offer independence and financial rewards for successful and responsible industrial safety and health technicians.

EARNINGS

According to the U.S. Department of Labor, the median annual salary of industrial safety and health technicians was $42,160 in 2006. The lowest 10 percent earned less than $25,240, and the highest 10 percent earned more than $68,640. In local government, safety and health technicians had mean annual earnings of $41,890.

Recent graduates in the safety sciences receive average starting salaries of $40,000 a year or more. According to a 2005 survey by *Safety+Health* magazine, nearly half of all respondents with between five and 10 years of experience reported earning between $50,000 and $79,999 annually. As they advance, top safety professionals with more than 20 years of experience can earn salaries of $100,000 or more.

Individuals in this career can expect benefits such as paid vacation, insurance, and paid holidays equal to those for other salaried employees in an organization. Some employers provide a special compensation plan for the industrial safety and health staff, including an annual bonus for measurably improving the company's safety record. In addition, technicians and other safety workers often find that employers provide liberal support for job-related study and professional programs. This may include paid memberships in professional organizations, travel, and other costs associated with attending meetings or conferences.

WORK ENVIRONMENT

Industrial safety and health technicians work either in an office or in the part of the plant for which they are responsible. Regardless of where they work, technicians must always set a good example for safety. When appropriate, they must wear safety clothes, hats, shoes, glasses, and other protective clothing, and of course, they must follow good safety practices at all times.

Technicians usually work during the day, but in plants that operate three shifts, some evening and night hours may be necessary. Jobs in mining and oil drilling may require safety technicians to be present around the clock, with "on-and-off" work shifts. Rates of pay for such situations are usually higher than for regular eight-hour shifts.

Office work usually involves reading government regulations, filing reports, maintaining records, and studying planned changes in safety procedures. Such work is likely to be fairly routine.

Whether working as part of a team of safety professionals or as part of the organization's management, industrial safety and health technicians must be able to juggle many tasks and coordinate with people in all departments. They must be able to communicate effectively with coworkers, union representatives, and supervisors. Technicians must also be effective teachers, able to impart information and instill a "safety first" attitude in others. Safe work habits are not acquired naturally. Industrial safety and health technicians who help fellow employees to work safely at their best rate of productivity can derive great satisfaction from their work.

OUTLOOK

According to the *Occupational Outlook Handbook*, employment for industrial safety and health technicians is expected to grow about as fast as the average for all occupations through 2014. While much of the demand for these technicians is created by industrial employers and their insurers, the overall demand is affected by the level of government regulation and enforcement regarding safety and health.

Over the last decade, there has been a general pullback in government regulation and spending on industrial safety and health. If this trend continues, employment levels will probably grow slowly, since approximately 40 percent of all safety specialists and technicians are employed by federal, state, and local governments.

In private industry, employment growth will be helped by the self-enforcement of company regulations and policies. Regardless of economic fluctuations, workers demanding a safe work environment will require the expertise of industrial safety and health technicians.

FOR MORE INFORMATION

For information on certification, contact
American Board of Industrial Hygiene
6015 West St. Joseph, Suite 102
Lansing, MI 48917-3980
Tel: 517-321-2638
Email: abih@abih.org
http://www.abih.org

For information on careers and training programs, contact
American Society of Safety Engineers
1800 East Oakton Street
Des Plaines, IL 60018-2100
Tel: 847-699-2929
Email: customerservice@asse.org
http://www.asse.org

For information on certification and to download copies of the Career Guide to the Safety Profession *and* Career Paths in Safety, *visit the BCSP's Web site.*
Board of Certified Safety Professionals (BCSP)
208 Burwash Avenue
Savoy, IL 61874-9571
Tel: 217-359-9263
Email: bcsp@bcsp.org
http://www.bcsp.com

For information on industrial safety issues, contact
Occupational Safety and Health Administration
U.S. Department of Labor
200 Constitution Avenue, NW
Washington, DC 20210-0001

Tel: 800-321-6742
http://www.osha.gov

For a variety of resources about industrial safety, contact
Industrial Accident Prevention Association
The Centre for Health & Safety Innovation
5110 Creekbank Road, Suite 300
Mississauga, ON L4W 0A1 Canada
Tel: 800-406-4272
http://www.iapa.on.ca

Machine Tool Operators

OVERVIEW

Machine tool operators operate or tend one or more types of machine tools that have already been set up for a job. These tools cut, drill, grind, bore, mill, or use a combination of methods to cut or finish pieces of metal or plastic products. These machines include lathes, boring mills, drilling and screw machines, jig grinders and borers, and milling machines. Some machine tool operators work with numerically controlled equipment.

HISTORY

At one time, before modern manufacturing procedures, goods were made individually by one craftsworker. As shops grew larger and employed more workers, the process changed. The steps involved in creating a product were separated into a series of easy tasks, which workers could learn quickly and do repetitively. Each worker was responsible for one part of the process.

Various tools were used in the manufacturing process, even in early times. One of the earliest machine tools, the wood lathe, actually dates back to ancient times and is probably a variation of the potter's wheel. It performs by mechanically rotating a workpiece against a stationary cutting tool.

With the advent of the industrial revolution, machine tools became more advanced and more widely used. During this time, lathes were adapted for cutting metal, and by the late 1700s, British inventor Henry Maudslay had devised the first

QUICK FACTS

School Subjects
Mathematics
Technical/shop

Personal Skills
Mechanical/manipulative
Technical/scientific

Work Environment
Primarily indoors
Primarily one location

Minimum Education Level
High school diploma

Salary Range
$20,600 to $31,670 to
$46,690+

Certification or Licensing
None available

Outlook
Decline

DOT
601

GOE
08.04.01

NOC
9511

O*NET-SOC
51-4021.00, 51-4022.00,
51-4023.00, 51-4031.00,
51-4032.00, 51-4033.00,
51-4034.00, 51-4035.00,
51-4072.00, 51-4081.00,
51-4191.01, 51-4193.00

screw-cutting lathe of high quality. By 1775, British industrialist John Wilkinson had invented a boring machine that made holes in metal with precise accuracy. The planer, a metal-cutting device that holds a workpiece in place while a cutting tool moves back and forth, was developed 25 years later. The planing tool allowed holes and flat surfaces to be smoothed to necessary degrees.

Technological improvements in machine tools affected the burgeoning industrial revolution. The use of such tools was, in fact, responsible in part for the design of early mass-production methods in the United States. However, the most rapid spurt in the development of machine tools has come since World Wars I and II. During the wars, it was necessary to build tanks, planes, jeeps, ships, and guns rapidly and accurately, so machines had to be devised that would turn out the thousands of pieces required.

The latest developments began in the 1950s and 1960s with the design of numerically controlled machine tools. A numerical control system regulates the performance of a machine tool by interpreting coded numerical data, which then directs the positioning and actual machining of the tool. Further improvements in machine tools have paralleled the advances in computer technology. Methods from which machine tooling has benefited include computer-integrated manufacturing, computer-aided design, and robotics.

THE JOB

Machine tool operators tend to the operation of one or two machines that have already been set up by a *job setter* or *setup operator.* Although some workers are known by the specific machines for which they are responsible (e.g., *lathe operator, drilling machine operator*), most are trained to work on a variety of machines.

A typical machine tool operator, for example, may tend a drilling machine. The operator starts the drill, inserts a piece of metal stock into the guide that holds it during machining, pulls down the lever of the drill press until the piece is drilled the prescribed distance, and releases the lever. Completed parts are then removed from the machine and placed in a bin.

During the machining process, the operator watches to make sure that the machine is working properly. When needed, the operator adds coolants and lubricants to the machinery and the workpiece. Except during breakdowns or while new stock is being brought up for machining, the machine tool operator generally repeats the same process until the batch of pieces is completed.

In some shops, though, an operator tends a series of the machines that shape and finish a machine part, and may even do some programming. Skill requirements vary from job to job. When a new program is loaded, it often must be adjusted to obtain the desired results. A *machinist* or *tool programmer* usually performs this function.

Because numerical control (NC) machine tools are expensive, operators who work on these more advanced machines carefully monitor operations to prevent costly damage to cutting tools or other parts. The extent to which this is required, however, depends on the type of job and equipment being used. In some cases, the operator may only need to watch a machine as it functions, and therefore can set up and operate more than one machine at a time. Other jobs may require frequent loading and unloading, tool changing, or programming. Operators check finished parts with micrometers, gauges, or other precision inspection equipment to ensure they meet specifications, although NC machine tools are increasingly performing this function as parts are produced.

REQUIREMENTS

High School
A high school diploma is preferred by most employers of machine tool operators. Classes in algebra, geometry, and drafting or mechanical drawing are excellent preparation for this job. Machine shop classes are also helpful.

Postsecondary Training
Most workers in this occupation learn their skills on the job. Trainees begin by observing and helping experienced workers, sometimes in formal training programs. As part of their training, they advance to more difficult and complex tasks, such as adjusting feed speeds or changing cutting tools. They also learn to check gauges and do basic shop calculations. Eventually, they become responsible for their own machines.

Other Requirements
If you are interested in this work, you should have better than average mechanical aptitude and manual dexterity and an interest in machines. The ability to pay close attention to a task, even when it becomes repetitive and dull, is essential. As machinery becomes more complex and shop floor organization changes, employers are increasingly looking for people with good communication skills.

Because machine tool operators spend most of their day standing at machines, you should have a certain amount of physical stamina.

EXPLORING

Hobbies such as building models and working with wood and other materials provide practical experience in fundamental machining concepts. If you want to explore the occupation further, high school or vocational school shop classes teach technical theory and machining techniques. You might join a student organization, such as SkillsUSA (http://www.skillsusa.org) or the Technology Student Association (http://www.tsaweb.org), if one is active at your school. If you wish to see machine tool operators in action, you can ask your teacher or guidance counselor to set up a visit to a local plant or you can investigate a summer or part-time job as a general helper in a nearby shop.

EMPLOYERS

According to the U.S. Department of Labor, approximately 91 percent of machine tool operators are employed in manufacturing industries—primarily in fabricated metal product manufacturing, plastics and rubber products manufacturing, primary metal manufacturing, machinery manufacturing, and motor vehicle parts manufacturing. Shops and plants are most often found in the industrial areas of the Northeast and Midwest as well as California.

STARTING OUT

Job seekers should apply directly to the personnel offices of machine shops and factories. Entry-level workers start out by doing a wide variety of jobs at the plant, first learning skills by observing experienced workers, and later by working under supervision until they are capable of working independently. This type of training usually lasts about one to two years. Job openings for machine tool operators are often listed in classified ads of newspapers as well as with state and private employment agencies.

ADVANCEMENT

Becoming a professional, skilled operator with commensurate wages often takes a number of years. In addition, it is generally only after several years' experience that a machine tool operator can advance to the position of setup operator. An operator who can read blueprints and use measurement tools, and who is willing to try new methods, is more likely to be moved into a supervisory job or to a more versatile position such as a numerical control programmer or a job setter. Operators may also transfer to training programs for other related occupations, such as precision machinist or toolmaker.

EARNINGS

The annual wage for machine tool operators varies according to which machines they run, the size of the facility, and where it is located. According to the U.S. Department of Labor, annual wages in 2006 ranged from less than $20,600 to $46,690 or more, depending on the position. Many workers often work more than 40 hours a week and earn overtime pay. Earnings also vary considerably by industry. Operators who work in the manufacturing of transportation equipment earn substantially more than those who work in rubber and plastic products manufacturing.

Many machine tool firms have traditional benefit plans, including retirement programs to which both the employer and the employee contribute. Most operators are also eligible for paid vacations, sick leave, and group hospitalization insurance.

In many manufacturing operations, the plant closes for a period of time to change over machinery in order to make new models. Workers are seldom paid for this downtime.

WORK ENVIRONMENT

In general, machine tool operators work a standard 40-hour week, but often, when large orders have to be met quickly, they may be asked to work late and on Saturdays. Work is performed exclusively indoors. Conditions can be somewhat dangerous, particularly because of the high speeds and pressures at which these machines operate. Therefore, protective equipment must be used, and safety rules must be observed. There are other minor hazards as well, including, for example, skin irritations from coolants used on cutting and drilling machines. Operators must wear goggles and avoid wearing loose clothing that could get caught in machinery. Most machine shops are clean, well lit, and ventilated, although some older ones may be less so. The shops are often noisy because of the operating machinery.

The main drawback to this profession is the repetitive and sometimes boring nature of the work. Machine tool operators typically spend hours each day performing the same task, over and over.

However, the fairly high wage for work that is relatively easy to learn and perform may compensate for the tedium of the job.

OUTLOOK

Employment of machine tool operators is expected to decline through 2014, according to the *Occupational Outlook Handbook*. The main reason is the change to labor-saving machinery. In order to remain competitive, many firms have adopted new technologies such as computer-controlled machine tools to improve quality and lower production costs. Computer-controlled equipment allows operators to tend a greater number of machines simultaneously, and thereby reduces the number of employees needed. However, employment of operators who are skilled in the use of these machines is expected to increase, while positions for manual machine operators continue to decline.

Also, the demand for machine tool operators parallels the demand for the products they produce. In recent years, plastic has been substituted for metal in many manufacturing parts. If this trend continues, the demand for machine tool operators in plastics manufacturing will be greater than for those in metals. The U.S. Department of Labor predicts that employment opportunities will also be better for multiple-machine-tool operators and molding, coremaking, and casting-machine operators, metal and plastic. Employment declines are expected for metal-refining furnace operators and tenders and pourers and casters, metal.

Even with the slow growth and decline in certain positions, there should be many job possibilities for machine operators. It is estimated that within the next 10 years, 60 percent of the existing workforce will be leaving the occupation due to expected retirements and will have to be replaced.

FOR MORE INFORMATION

For information on training and jobs for machine tool operators, contact

International Union, United Automobile, Aerospace, and
    Agricultural Implement Workers of America
Skilled Trades Department
8000 East Jefferson Avenue
Detroit, MI 48214-3963
Tel: 313-926-5000
http://www.uaw.org

International Union of Electronic, Electrical, Salaried,
   Machine, and Furniture Workers-Communications Workers
   of America
301 Third Street, NW
Washington, DC 20001
http://www.iue-cwa.org

*For literature on training and careers in the machine tools trades,
contact*
National Tooling and Machining Association
9300 Livingston Road
Fort Washington, MD 20744-4914
Tel: 800-248-6862
http://www.ntma.org

Precision Machined Products Association
6700 West Snowville Road
Brecksville, OH 44141-3212
Tel: 440-526-0300
http://www.pmpa.org

*For useful resources about careers and internships in the metalform-
ing industry, contact*
Precision Metalforming Association Educational Foundation
6363 Oak Tree Boulevard
Independence, OH 44131-2500
Tel: 216-901-8800
Email: pmaef@pma.org
http://www.pmaef.org

For industry information, contact
Tooling and Manufacturing Association (TMA)
1177 South Dee Road
Park Ridge, IL 60068-4379
Tel: 847-825-1120
http://www.tmanet.org

Manufacturing Supervisors

OVERVIEW

Manufacturing supervisors monitor employees and their working conditions and effectiveness in production plants and factories. They ensure that work is carried out correctly and on schedule by promoting high product quality and output levels. In addition to balancing the budget and other bookkeeping duties, supervisors are responsible for maintaining employee work schedules, training new workers, and issuing warnings to workers who violate established rules. Manufacturing managers in various industries hold approximately 160,000 jobs.

HISTORY

Manufacturing has been through many technological developments, from innovations in fuel-powered machinery to the assembly line. As these processes became more complex, no single worker could be responsible for the production of particular items. Manufacturing became a long process involving many workers' contributions. If one worker caused a defect in the product, it was not always easy to track down the source of the problem. The role of the supervisor emerged as a means of keeping track of the work of numerous employees involved in the production process, allowing production to run smoothly.

THE JOB

The primary roles of manufacturing supervisors are to oversee their employees and ensure the effectiveness of the production process.

A manufacturing supervisor discusses the day's production with a group of workers. *(Bob Daemmrich, The Image Works)*

They are responsible for the amount of work and the quality of work being done by the employees under their direction. Supervisors make work schedules, keep production and employee records, and plan on-the-job activities. Their work is highly interpersonal. They not only monitor employees, but also guide workers in their efforts and are responsible for disciplining and counseling poor performers as well as recommending valuable employees for raises and promotions. They also make sure that safety regulations and other rules and procedures are being followed.

In monitoring production and output levels, manufacturing supervisors must keep in mind the company's limitations, such as budgetary allowances, time constraints, and any workforce shortages. They must be realistic about the abilities of their employees and set production schedules accordingly. Supervisors may use mathematical calculations and test various production methods to reach high production levels while still maintaining the quality of the product.

Manufacturing supervisors may be employed by small companies, such as custom furniture shops, or large industrial factories, such as automotive plants. Supervisors report to company managers, who direct them on production goals and set budgets. Another important part of the supervisor's job is to act as a liaison between factory workers and company managers who are in charge of production. Supervisors announce new company policies and plans to the workers in their charge and report to their managers any problems they may be having or other important issues. Supervisors also may meet with other company supervisors to discuss progress toward company objectives, department operations, and employee performance. In companies where employees belong to labor unions, supervisors must know and follow all work-related guidelines outlined by labor-management contracts.

REQUIREMENTS

High School

If you are interested in becoming a manufacturing supervisor, take high school courses in business, math, and science to prepare for the demands of the job. In order to balance the budget and determine production schedules, supervisors often use mathematical computations. They also use computers to do much of their paperwork, so take any available classes to become familiar with word processing and spreadsheet programs.

Postsecondary Training

Because manufacturing areas differ, there is no single path to a supervisory position. However, most manufacturing supervisors hold a college degree in business administration or industrial management. College courses in business, industrial relations, math, and computer applications help to familiarize prospective supervisors with the many responsibilities they will have to handle. Interpersonal skills are also highly valuable so classes in public relations and human resource management are also important.

Many supervisors obtain graduate degrees to become more marketable to employers or for a better chance of advancing within a company. As manufacturing processes have become more complex, advanced degrees in business administration, engineering, or industrial management are more and more common among those in higher-level positions.

Other Requirements

Manufacturing supervisors deal with many people on a highly personal level. They must direct, guide, and discipline others, so you should work on developing strong leadership qualities. You will also need good communication skills and the ability to motivate people and maintain morale.

EXPLORING

To better gauge your interest and expand your knowledge about manufacturing careers, ask your school's guidance counselor for advice on setting up a tour of a local production factory or plant. At the factory or plant, you might be able to talk to workers about their jobs or at least see the environment in which they work. Simply reading more about the field of manufacturing and its many different employment opportunities is also a good way to explore this career. Visit your local library or surf the Internet for recent articles and information.

A summer or part-time job in an office or retail setting can give you business experience and expose you to management practices. Depending on the job and industry, perhaps you might even be promoted to an assistant manager position.

EMPLOYERS

There are approximately 160,000 manufacturing supervisors working all over the United States, but the majority of jobs are located in highly industrial areas. Whether it be in a small production facility or a large factory or plant, supervisors are needed to oversee all manufacturing processes. The major employment areas are industrial machinery and equipment, semiconductor and other electronic components, plastics products, transportation equipment, motor vehicle parts, electronic and electrical equipment, metal instruments and related products, printing and related services, and food industries. A small number of these managers are self-employed.

STARTING OUT

Many supervisors enter their jobs by moving up from factory worker positions. They may also apply for supervisory positions from outside the company. Companies that hire manufacturing supervisors look for experience, knowledge of the job or industry, organizational skills, and leadership abilities. Supervisory positions may be found in classified ads, but for those just looking to get started, part-time or full-time jobs in a factory setting may help provide some experience and familiarity with the work of supervisors.

ADVANCEMENT

In most manufacturing companies, an advanced degree in business management or administration along with accumulated work experience is the best method for advancement into higher level supervisory positions. From the position of supervisor, one may advance to manager or head of an entire manufacturing plant or factory.

EARNINGS

Salaries for manufacturing supervisors vary depending on the factory or plant in which they work, the area of production that they supervise, and their years of experience in the position. The U.S. Department of Labor reports that the median annual salary for manufacturing supervisors was $77,670 in 2006. The lowest 10 percent earned less than $47,230, and the highest 10 percent earned more than $130,680.

Manufacturing supervisors typically receive benefits such as retirement plans, medical and life insurance, and paid holidays and vacations.

WORK ENVIRONMENT

Most supervisors work on the manufacturing or factory floor. They may be on their feet most of the time, which can be tiring, and work near loud and hazardous machines. Supervisors may begin their day early so that they arrive before their workers, and they may stay later than their workers. Some may work for plants that operate around the clock and may work overnight shifts, weekends, and holidays. Sometimes the best hours go to those who have been with the company the longest. Plant downsizing and restructuring often leads to fewer supervisors. As a result, manufacturing supervisors may face larger departments to oversee and other increased demands.

OUTLOOK

To some extent, the future of the manufacturing supervisor job depends on the individual industry, whether it be automobiles or food products. In manufacturing as a whole, employment of supervisors is expected to grow more slowly than the average for all occupations through 2014, as supervisors have begun to oversee more workers. Corporate downsizing and the use of computers for tasks such as producing production schedules and budget plans also require fewer supervisors than before. However, there will be a need to replace job-changing or retiring managers. Job candidates with higher levels of education (especially those with an undergraduate engineering degree and a master's degree in business administration or industrial management) and related work experience will fare the best in landing a supervisory position.

FOR MORE INFORMATION

For information on workplace trends and management and leadership training, contact
American Management Association
1601 Broadway
New York, NY 10019-7434
Tel: 212-586-8100
http://www.amanet.org

For general information on manufacturing careers, industry news, and training tools, contact
National Association of Manufacturers
1331 Pennsylvania Avenue, NW
Washington, DC 20004-1790
Tel: 202-637-3000
Email: manufacturing@nam.org
http://www.nam.org

For useful information on manufacturing careers, contact
GetTech.org
http://www.gettech.org

Mechanical Engineering Technicians

OVERVIEW

Mechanical engineering technicians work under the direction of mechanical engineers to design, build, maintain, and modify many kinds of machines, mechanical devices, and tools. They work in a wide range of industries and in a variety of specific jobs within every industry.

Mechanical engineering technicians review mechanical drawings and project instructions, analyze design plans to determine costs and practical value, sketch rough layouts of proposed machines or parts, assemble new or modified devices or components, test completed assemblies or components, analyze test results, and write reports. There are approximately 48,000 mechanical engineering technicians employed in the United States.

HISTORY

Mechanical engineering dates back to ancient times, when it was used almost exclusively for military purposes. The Romans were the first to use the science for nonmilitary projects, such as aqueducts, roads, and bridges, although many if not most of these structures were built to advance military objectives.

With the advent of the industrial revolution and the use of machines for manufacturing, mechanical engineering technology took a giant step forward. One of the most important figures in this revolution was Eli Whitney. Having received a government contract in 1798 to produce 15,000 muskets, he hired not gunsmiths, but mechanics. At that time, all articles, including muskets, were built one by one by individual craftsworkers. No two muskets were ever alike.

Whitney took a different approach. For two years after receiving the contract, he focused on developing and building special-purpose machines, and then trained mechanics to make specific parts of the gun. When he was finished, Whitney had invented new machine tools and attachments, such as the milling machine and jig, made real the concept of interchangeable parts, and paved the way for the modern manufacturing assembly line.

This manufacturing process required not only ingenious inventors and skilled mechanics to operate the machines, but also skilled assistants to help develop new machines, set or reset tolerances, maintain and repair operational equipment, and direct, supervise, and instruct workers. These assistants are today's mechanical engineering technicians, a crucial part of the engineering team. In addition to manufacturing, they are employed in almost every application that uses mechanical principles.

THE JOB

Mechanical engineering technicians are employed in a broad range of industries. Technicians may specialize in any one of many areas including biomedical equipment, measurement and control, products manufacturing, solar energy, turbo machinery, energy resource technology, and engineering materials and technology.

Within each application, a technician may be involved with various aspects of the work. One phase is research and development. In this area, the mechanical technician may assist an engineer or scientist in the design and development of anything from a ballpoint pen to a sophisticated measuring device. These technicians prepare rough sketches and layouts of the project being developed.

In the design of an automobile engine, for example, engineering technicians make drawings that detail the fans, pistons, connecting rods, and flywheels to be used in the engine. They estimate cost and operational qualities of each part, taking into account friction, stress, strain, and vibration. By performing these tasks, they free the engineer to accomplish other research activities.

A second common type of work for mechanical engineering technicians is testing. For products such as engines, motors, or other moving devices, technicians may set up prototypes of the equipment to be tested and run performance tests. Some tests require one procedure to be done repeatedly, while others require that equipment be

Mechanical engineering technicians should have the ability to use hand and power tools and carry out detailed work. *(Dick Blume, Syracuse Newspapers/The Image Works)*

run over long periods of time to observe any changes in operation. Technicians collect and compile all necessary data from the testing procedures and prepare reports for the engineer or scientist.

In order to manufacture a product, preparations must be made for its production. In this effort, mechanical engineering technicians assist in the product design by making final design layouts and detailed drawings of parts to be manufactured and of any special manufacturing equipment needed. Some test and inspect machines and equipment or work with engineers to eliminate production problems.

Other mechanical engineering technicians examine plans and drawings to determine what materials are needed and prepare lists of these materials, specifying quality, size, and strength. They also may estimate labor costs, equipment life, and plant space needed. After the product is manufactured, some mechanical engineering technicians may help solve storage and shipping problems, while others assist in customer relations when product installation is required.

Some engineering technicians work with *tool designers*, who prepare sketches of designs for cutting tools, jigs, special fixtures, and other devices used in mass production. Frequently, they redesign existing tools to improve their efficiency.

REQUIREMENTS

High School

Preparation for this career begins in high school. Although entrance requirements to associate's degree programs vary somewhat from school to school, mathematics and physical science form the backbone of a good preparatory curriculum. Classes should include algebra, geometry, science, computer science, mechanical drawing, shop, and communications.

Postsecondary Training

Associate's degree or two-year mechanical technician programs are designed to prepare students for entry-level positions. Most programs accredited by the Accreditation Board for Engineering and Technology offer one year of basic training with a chance to specialize in the second year. The first year of the program generally consists of courses in college algebra and trigonometry, science, and communication skills. Other classes introduce students to the manufacturing processes, drafting, and language of the industry.

The second-year courses focus on mechanical technology. These include fluid mechanics, thermodynamics, tool and machine design, instruments and controls, production technology, electricity, and electronics. Many schools allow their students to choose a major in the second year of the program, which provides training for a specific area of work in the manufacturing industry.

Certification or Licensing

Many mechanical engineering technicians choose to become certified by the National Institute for Certification in Engineering Technologies. To become certified, a technician must combine a specific amount of job-related experience with a written examination. Certifications are offered at several levels of expertise. Such certification is generally voluntary, although obtaining certification shows a high level of commitment and dedication that employers find highly desirable.

Mechanical engineering technicians are encouraged to become affiliated with professional groups, such as the American Society of Certified Engineering Technicians, that offer continuing education sessions for members. Some mechanical engineering technicians may be required to belong to unions.

Other Requirements

To work as a mechanical engineering technician, you need mathematical and mechanical aptitude. You will need to understand abstract concepts and apply scientific principles to problems in the shop or laboratory, in both the design and the manufacturing process. You should be interested in people and machines and have the ability to carry out detailed work. You should be able to analyze sketches and drawings and possess patience, perseverance, and resourcefulness. Additionally, you must have good communication skills and be able to present both spoken and written reports.

EXPLORING

You may be able to obtain part-time or summer work in a machine shop or factory. This type of work usually consists of sweeping floors and clearing out machine tools, but it will also give you an opportunity to view the field firsthand and demonstrates your interest to future employers. Field trips to industrial laboratories, drafting studios, or manufacturing facilities can offer overall views of this type of work. Hobbies like automobile repair, model making, and electronic kit assembly can also be helpful. Finally, if you are in high school and interested in the engineering field, consider joining JETS, the Junior Engineering Technical Society.

EMPLOYERS

Many of the 48,000 mechanical engineering technicians employed in the United States work in durable goods manufacturing, primarily making electrical and electronic machinery and equipment, industrial machinery and equipment, instruments and related products, and transportation equipment. A sizable percentage work in service industries, mostly in engineering and business services companies that do contract work for government, manufacturing, and other organizations.

The federal government employs mechanical engineering technicians in the Departments of Defense, Transportation, Agriculture, and Interior, as well as the Tennessee Valley Authority and the National Aeronautics and Space Administration. State and municipal governments also employ mechanical engineering technicians.

STARTING OUT

Schools offering associate's degrees in mechanical engineering technology and two-year technician programs usually help graduates find employment. At most colleges, in fact, company recruiters interview prospective graduates during their final semester of school. As a result, many students receive job offers before graduation. Other graduates may prefer to apply directly to employers, use newspaper classified ads, or apply through public or private employment services.

ADVANCEMENT

As mechanical engineering technicians remain with a company, they become more valuable to the employer. Opportunities for advancement are available to those who are willing to accept greater responsibilities either by specializing in a specific field, taking on more technically complex assignments, or by assuming supervisory duties. Some technicians advance by moving into technical sales or customer relations. Mechanical technicians who further their education may choose to become tool designers or mechanical engineers.

EARNINGS

Salaries for mechanical engineering technicians vary depending on the nature and location of the job, employer, amount of training the technician has received, and number of years of experience.

According to the U.S. Department of Labor, the median annual salary for mechanical engineering technicians was $45,850 in 2006. In general, mechanical engineering technicians who develop and test machinery and equipment under the direction of an engineering staff earn between $30,000 and $50,000 a year. Mechanical engineering technicians at the start of their careers earned around $25,000 a year or less, while senior technicians with specialized skills and experience earned much more, between $50,000 and $70,000 a year.

These salaries are based upon the standard 40-hour workweek. Overtime or premium time pay may be earned for work beyond regular daytime hours or workweek. Other benefits, depending on the company and union agreements, include paid vacation days, insurance, retirement plans, profit sharing, and tuition-reimbursement plans.

WORK ENVIRONMENT

Mechanical engineering technicians work in a variety of conditions, depending on their field of specialization. Technicians who specialize in design may find that they spend most of their time at the drafting board or computer. Those who specialize in manufacturing may spend some time at a desk, but also spend considerable time in manufacturing areas or shops.

Conditions also vary by industry. Some industries require technicians to work in foundries, die-casting rooms, machine shops, assembly areas, or punch-press areas. Most of these areas, however, are well lighted, heated, and ventilated. Moreover, most industries employing mechanical engineering technicians have strong safety programs.

Mechanical engineering technicians are often called upon to exercise decision-making skills, to be responsible for valuable equipment, and to act as effective leaders. At other times they carry out routine, uncomplicated tasks. Similarly, in some cases, they may coordinate the activities of others, while at other times, they are the ones supervised. They must be able to respond well to both types of demands. In return for this flexibility and versatility, mechanical engineering technicians are usually highly respected by their employers and coworkers.

OUTLOOK

Job opportunities for mechanical engineering technicians are expected to grow about as fast as the average for all occupations through 2014, according to the U.S. Department of Labor. Manufacturing companies will be looking for more ways to apply the advances in mechanical technology to their operations. Opportunities will be best for technicians who are skilled in new manufacturing concepts, materials, and designs. Many job openings also will be created by people retiring or leaving the field.

However, the employment outlook for engineering technicians is influenced by the economy. Hiring will fluctuate with the ups and downs of the nation's overall economic situation.

FOR MORE INFORMATION

For information on colleges and universities offering accredited programs in engineering technology, contact
Accreditation Board for Engineering and Technology
111 Market Place, Suite 1050
Baltimore, MD 21202-7116
Tel: 410-347-7700
http://www.abet.org

For information about membership in this professional society for engineering technicians, contact
American Society of Certified Engineering Technicians
PO Box 1536
Brandon, MS 39043-1356
Tel: 601-824-8991
Email: General-Manager@ascet.org
http://www.ascet.org

For information about the field of mechanical engineering, contact
American Society of Mechanical Engineers
Three Park Avenue
New York, NY 10016-5990
Tel: 800-843-2763
Email: infocentral@asme.org
http://www.asme.org

For information on technician careers and high school programs that provide opportunities to learn about engineering technology, contact
Junior Engineering Technical Society
1420 King Street, Suite 405
Alexandria, VA 22314-2794
Tel: 703-548-5387
Email: info@jets.org
http://www.jets.org

For information on certification, contact
National Institute for Certification in Engineering Technologies
1420 King Street
Alexandria, VA 22314-2794
Tel: 888-476-4238
http://www.nicet.org

Mechanical Engineers

OVERVIEW

Mechanical engineers plan and design tools, engines, machines, and other mechanical systems that produce, transmit, or use power. They may work in design, instrumentation, testing, robotics, transportation, or bioengineering, among other areas. The broadest of all engineering disciplines, mechanical engineering extends across many interdependent specialties. Mechanical engineers may work in production operations, maintenance, or technical sales, and many are administrators or managers. There are approximately 226,000 mechanical engineers employed in the United States.

HISTORY

The modern field of mechanical engineering took root during the Renaissance. In this period, engineers focused their energies on developing more efficient ways to perform such ordinary tasks as grinding grain and pumping water. Water wheels and windmills were common energy producers at that time. Leonardo da Vinci, who attempted to design such complex machines as a submarine and a helicopter, best personified the burgeoning mechanical inventiveness of the period. One of the Renaissance's most significant inventions was the mechanical clock, powered first by falling weights and later by compressed springs.

Despite these developments, it was not until the industrial revolution that mechanical engineering took on its modern form. The steam engine, an efficient power producer, was introduced in 1712

QUICK FACTS

School Subjects
Computer science
English
Mathematics

Personal Skills
Leadership/management
Technical/scientific

Work Environment
Primarily indoors
One location with some
travel

Minimum Education Level
Bachelor's degree

Salary Range
$45,170 to $69,850 to
$104,900+

Certification or Licensing
Voluntary (certification)
Required by all states
(licensing)

Outlook
About as fast as the average

DOT
007

GOE
02.07.04

NOC
2132

O*NET-SOC
17-2141.00

by Thomas Newcomen to pump water from English mines. More than a half century later, James Watt modified Newcomen's engine to power industrial machines. In 1876, a German, Nicolaus Otto, developed the internal combustion engine, which became one of the century's most important inventions. In 1847, a group of British engineers who specialized in steam engines and machine tools organized the Institution of Mechanical Engineers. The American Society of Mechanical Engineers was founded in 1880.

Mechanical engineering rapidly expanded in the 20th century. Mass production systems allowed large quantities of standardized goods to be made at a low cost, and mechanical engineers played a pivotal role in the design of these systems. In the second half of the 20th century, computers revolutionized production. Mechanical engineers now design mechanical systems on computers, and they are used to test, monitor, and analyze mechanical systems and factory production. Mechanical engineers are key players in countless industries, including the aviation and aerospace industries.

THE JOB

The work of mechanical engineering begins with research and development. A company may need to develop a more fuel-efficient automobile engine, for example, or a cooling system for air-conditioning and refrigeration that does not harm the earth's atmosphere. A research engineer explores the project's theoretical, mechanical, and material problems. The engineer may perform experiments to gather necessary data and acquire new knowledge. Often, an experimental device or system is developed.

The *design engineer* takes information gained from research and development and uses it to plan a commercially useful product. To prevent rotting in a grain storage system, for example, a design engineer might use research on a new method of circulating air through grain. The engineer would be responsible for specifying every detail of the machine or mechanical system. Since the introduction of sophisticated software programs, mechanical engineers have increasingly used computers in the design process.

After the product has been designed and a prototype developed, the product is analyzed by *testing engineers*. A tractor transmission, for example, would need to be tested for temperature, vibration, dust, and performance under the required loads, as well as for any government safety regulations. If dust is penetrating a bearing, the testing engineer would refer the problem to the design engineer, who would then make an adjustment to the design of the transmission.

Design and testing engineers continue to work together until the product meets the necessary criteria.

Once the final design is set, it is the job of the *manufacturing engineer* to come up with the most time- and cost-efficient way of making the product without sacrificing quality. The amount of factory floor space, the type of manufacturing equipment and machinery, and the cost of labor and materials are some of the factors that must be considered. Engineers select the necessary equipment and machines and oversee their arrangement and safe operation. Other engineering specialists, such as chemical, electrical, and industrial engineers, may provide assistance.

Some types of mechanical systems (from factory machinery to nuclear power plants) are so sophisticated that mechanical engineers are needed for operation and ongoing maintenance. With the help of computers, *maintenance and operations engineers* use their specialized knowledge to monitor complex production systems and make necessary adjustments.

Mechanical engineers also work in marketing, sales, and administration. Because of their training in mechanical engineering, *sales engineers* can give customers a detailed explanation of how a machine or system works. They may also be able to alter its design to meet a customer's needs.

In a small company, a mechanical engineer may need to perform many, if not most, of the above responsibilities. Some tasks might be assigned to *consulting engineers*, who are either self-employed or work for a consulting firm.

Other mechanical engineers may work in a number of specialized areas. *Energy specialists* work with power production machines to supply clean and efficient energy to individuals and industries. *Application engineers* specialize in computer-aided design systems. *Process engineers* work in environmental sciences to reduce air pollution levels without sacrificing essential services such as those provided by power stations or utility companies.

REQUIREMENTS

High School

If you are interested in mechanical engineering as a career, you need to take courses in geometry, trigonometry, and calculus. Physics and chemistry courses are also recommended, as is mechanical drawing or computer-aided design, if they are offered at your high school. Communication skills are important for mechanical engineers because they interact with a variety of coworkers and vendors and are often required to prepare and/or present reports. English and speech classes are also helpful. Finally, because computers are such an important part of engineering, computer science courses are good choices.

Postsecondary Training

A bachelor's degree in mechanical engineering is usually the minimum educational requirement for entering this field. A master's degree, or even a Ph.D., may be necessary to obtain some positions, such as those in research, teaching, and administration.

In the United States, there are more than 280 colleges and universities where the Accreditation Board for Engineering and Technology has approved mechanical engineering programs. Although admissions requirements vary slightly from school to school, most require a solid background in mathematics and science.

In a four-year undergraduate program, students typically begin by studying mathematics and science subjects, such as calculus, differential equations, physics, and chemistry. Course work in liberal arts and elementary mechanical engineering is also taken. By the third year, students begin to study the technical core subjects of mechanical engineering—mechanics, thermodynamics, fluid mechanics, design manufacturing, and heat transfer—as well as such specialized topics as power generation and transmission, computer-aided design systems, and the properties of materials.

At some schools, a five- or six-year program combines classroom study with practical experience working for an engineering firm or a government agency such as the National Aeronautics and Space Administration (NASA). Although these cooperative, or work-study, programs take longer, they offer significant advantages. Not only does the salary help pay for educational expenses, but the student has the opportunity to apply theoretical knowledge to actual work problems in mechanical engineering. In some cases, the company or government agency may offer full-time employment to its co-op workers after graduation.

A graduate degree is a prerequisite for becoming a university professor or researcher. It may also lead to a higher-level job within an engineering department or firm. Some companies encourage their employees to pursue graduate education by offering tuition-reimbursement programs. Because technology is rapidly developing, mechanical engineers need to continue their education, formally or informally, throughout their careers. Conferences, seminars, and professional journals serve to educate engineers about developments in the field.

Certification or Licensing

Many mechanical engineers become certified. Certification is a status granted by a technical or professional organization for the purpose of recognizing and documenting an individual's abilities in a specific engineering field. For example, the Society of Manufacturing Engineers offers the following designations to mechanical engineers who work in manufacturing and who meet education and experience requirements: certified manufacturing engineer and certified engineer manager. Contact the society for more information on these certifications.

Engineers whose work may affect the life, health, or safety of the public must be registered according to regulations in all 50 states and the District of Columbia. Applicants for registration must have received a degree from an accredited engineering program and have four years of experience. They must also pass a written examination.

Other Requirements

Personal qualities essential for mechanical engineers include the ability to think analytically, to solve problems, and to work with abstract ideas. Attention to detail is also important, as are good oral and written communication skills and the ability to work well in groups. Computer literacy is essential.

EXPLORING

One of the best ways to learn about the field is to talk with a mechanical engineer. Public libraries usually have books on mechanical engineering that might be enlightening. You might tackle a design or building project to test your aptitude for the field. Finally, some high schools offer engineering clubs or organizations. Membership in JETS, the Junior Engineering Technical Society (http://www.jets. org), is suggested for prospective mechanical engineers.

EMPLOYERS

Approximately 226,000 mechanical engineers are employed in the United States. They work for private engineering and aerospace companies and government entities such as NASA and the U.S. Department of Defense. Mechanical engineers also work in a variety of other settings, including manufacturers of industrial and office machinery, farm equipment, automobiles, petroleum, pharmaceuticals, fabricated metal products, pulp and paper, electronics, utilities, computers, soap and cosmetics, and heating, ventilating, and air-conditioning systems all employ mechanical engineers. Others are self-employed or work for colleges and universities.

STARTING OUT

Many mechanical engineers find their first job through their college or university career services office. Many companies send recruiters to college campuses to interview and sign up engineering graduates. Other students might find a position in the company where they had a summer or part-time job. Newspapers and professional journals often list job openings for engineers.

ADVANCEMENT

As engineers gain experience, they can advance to jobs with a wider scope of responsibility and higher pay. Some of these higher-level jobs include technical service and development officers, team leaders, research directors, and managers. Some mechanical engineers use their technical knowledge in sales and marketing positions, while others form their own engineering business or consulting firm.

Many engineers advance by furthering their education. A master's degree in business administration, in addition to an engineering degree, is sometimes helpful in obtaining an administrative position. A master's or doctoral degree in an engineering specialty may also lead to executive work. In addition, those with graduate degrees often have the option of research or teaching positions.

EARNINGS

The National Association of Colleges and Employers reports the following 2005 starting salaries for mechanical engineers by educational achievement: bachelor's degree, $50,236; master's degree, $59,880; and Ph.D., $68,299. The U.S. Department of Labor reports that mechanical engineers had median annual salaries of $69,850 in 2006. Salaries ranged from less than $45,170 to $104,900 or more.

Like most professionals, mechanical engineers who work for a company or for a government agency usually receive a generous benefits package, including vacation days, sick leave, health and life insurance, and a savings and pension program. Self-employed mechanical engineers must provide their own benefits.

WORK ENVIRONMENT

The working conditions of mechanical engineers vary. Most mechanical engineers work indoors in offices, research laboratories, or production departments of factories and shops. Depending on the job, however, a significant amount of work time may be spent on a noisy factory floor, at a construction site, or at another field operation. Mechanical engineers have traditionally designed systems on drafting boards, but since the introduction of sophisticated software programs, design is increasingly done on computers.

Engineering is, for the most part, a cooperative effort. While the specific duties of an engineer may require independent work, each project is typically the job of an engineering team. Such a team might include other engineers, engineering technicians, and engineering technologists.

Mechanical engineers generally have a 40-hour workweek; however, their working hours are often dictated by project deadlines. They may work long hours to meet a deadline, or show up on a second or third shift to check production at a factory or a construction project.

Mechanical engineering can be a very satisfying occupation. Engineers often get the pleasure of seeing their designs or modifications put into actual, tangible form, such as a streamlined assembly line or a new type of spacecraft. Conversely, it can be frustrating when a project is stalled, full of errors, or even abandoned completely.

OUTLOOK

The employment of mechanical engineers is expected to grow about as fast as the average for all occupations through 2014, according to the U.S. Department of Labor. Although overall employment in manufacturing is expected to decline, engineers will be needed to meet the demand for more efficient industrial machinery and machine tools. The Department of Labor predicts good opportunities for mechanical engineers who are involved with new technologies such as biotechnology, nanotechnology, and materials science. It should also be noted that increases in defense spending in the wake of the terrorist attacks of September 11, 2001, might create improved employment opportunities for engineers within the federal government.

FOR MORE INFORMATION

For a list of engineering programs at colleges and universities, contact
Accreditation Board for Engineering and Technology
111 Market Place, Suite 1050
Baltimore, MD 21202-7116
Tel: 410-347-7700
http://www.abet.org

For information on mechanical engineering and mechanical engineering technology, contact
American Society of Mechanical Engineers
Three Park Avenue
New York, NY 10016-5990
Tel: 800-843-2763
Email: infocentral@asme.org
http://www.asme.org

For information about mechanical engineering careers and high school engineering competitions, contact
Junior Engineering Technical Society
1420 King Street, Suite 405
Alexandria, VA 22314-2794
Tel: 703-548-5387
Email: info@jets.org
http://www.jets.org

For information on certification, contact
Society of Manufacturing Engineers
One SME Drive
Dearborn, MI 48121-2408
Tel: 800-733-4763
http://www.sme.org

Millwrights

OVERVIEW

Millwrights install, assemble, and maintain heavy industrial machinery and other equipment. If necessary, they construct foundations for certain large assemblies. They may also dismantle, operate, or repair these machines. Approximately 59,000 millwrights are employed in the United States.

HISTORY

The history of the millwright dates back to the industrial revolution. While milling machines, power looms, drill presses, lathes, and other equipment made mass production of goods possible, these new machines were too complicated for the average worker to understand. It became necessary to assign workers with specialized training to install, maintain, and repair equipment. With the growth of industrial establishments and the increasing complexity of machines, the millwright became an integral part of the labor force.

THE JOB

Millwrights are highly skilled workers whose primary function is to install heavy machinery. When machinery arrives at the job site, it must be unloaded, inspected, and moved into position. For light machinery, millwrights use rigging and hoisting devices such as pulleys and cables to lift and position equipment. For heavier jobs, they are assisted by hydraulic lift-truck or crane operators. To decide what type of device is needed to position machinery, millwrights must know the load-bearing properties of ropes, cables, hoists, and cranes.

New machinery sometimes requires a new foundation. Millwrights either prepare the foundation themselves or supervise its construction. To do this, they must be able to work with concrete, wood, and steel, and read blueprints and schematic diagrams to make any electrical connections.

When installing machinery, millwrights fit bearings, align gears and wheels, attach motors, and connect belts according to the manufacturer's instructions. They may use hand and power tools, cutting torches, welding machines, and soldering guns. In order to modify parts to fit specifications, they use metalworking equipment such as lathes and grinders.

Millwrights must be very precise in their work and have good mathematical skills to measure angles, material thicknesses, and small distances with tools such as squares, calipers, and micrometers. When a high level of precision is required, such as on a production line, lasers may be used for alignment.

Once machinery is installed, millwrights may do repair or preventive maintenance work such as oiling and greasing parts and replacing worn components.

Millwrights may be hired to change the placement of existing machines in a plant or mill to set up a new production line or improve efficiency. Their contribution is key to the planning of complicated production processes. In large shops and plants, they may update machinery placement to improve the production process. They may

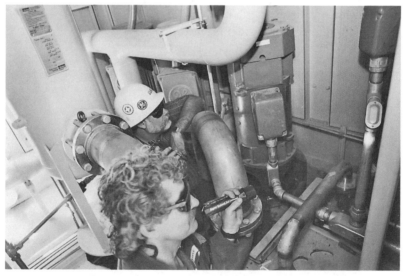

A millwright (wearing hard hat) and a millwright journeyman check the rotation of motors at a plant. *(Susan Goldman, The Image Works)*

even move and reassemble machinery each time a new production run starts. In smaller factories, however, machinery is rearranged only to increase production and improve efficiency. Millwrights consult with supervisors, planners, and engineers to determine the proper placement of equipment based on floor loads, workflow, safety measures, and other important concerns.

The increasing use of automation in many industries means that millwrights are responsible for installing and maintaining more sophisticated machines. When working with this more complicated machinery, millwrights are assisted by computer or electronic experts, electricians, and manufacturers' representatives.

REQUIREMENTS

High School
Employers prefer applicants with a high school diploma or equivalency. You should take courses in science, mathematics, and shop to give you a technical and mechanical foundation. Any class with an emphasis on mechanical reasoning, such as mechanical drawing, blueprint reading, hydraulics, and machine shop, is of particular value.

Postsecondary Training
Millwrights receive their training either through a formal apprenticeship program or through community colleges combined with informal on-the-job training. Apprenticeships last for four years and combine hands-on training with classroom instruction. During the program, apprentices gain experience dismantling, moving, erecting, and repairing machinery. They may also work with concrete and receive instruction in carpentry, welding, and sheet metal work. Classes focus on mathematics, blueprint reading, hydraulics, electricity, and computers.

Other Requirements
To handle the physical demands involved in the work, applicants should be in good health and physically fit. A high level of coordination and mechanical aptitude is necessary to read complicated diagrams and work with the machinery. Communication and interpersonal skills also are needed for giving instructions and working in teams.

EXPLORING

One of the best ways to find out more about this career is to talk with a working millwright. You should develop a list of questions to ask, such as details about the responsibilities, hours, pay, and how he or she first got into the work. You could also visit an industrial setting that employs millwrights to watch these workers in action. Local unions that represent millwrights can also provide you with information on the career.

EMPLOYERS

Millwrights work in every state but are concentrated in highly industrial areas. Most are employed in industries that manufacture durable goods, such as automobiles, steel, and metal products, or in construction. Others work in plants that manufacture paper, chemicals, knit goods, and other items, or with utility companies. Manufacturers and retailers of industrial machinery often employ millwrights, usually under contract, to install machines for their customers. There are approximately 59,000 millwrights employed in the United States.

STARTING OUT

The usual entry method is through an apprenticeship. Most apprentices start out with unskilled or semiskilled work in a plant or factory. As they gain experience and job openings become available, they move into positions requiring more skilled labor. Openings are generally filled according to experience and seniority.

ADVANCEMENT

Most advancement for millwrights comes in the form of higher wages. With the proper training, skill, and seniority, however, workers can move to supervisory positions or work as trainers for apprentices. Others may choose to become self-employed contractors.

EARNINGS

Millwrights are typically paid by the hour. According to the U.S. Department of Labor, hourly earnings averaged $21.94 (or $45,630 annually) in 2006. The lowest 10 percent earned less than $13.84 an hour (or $28,790 annually) and the highest 10 percent earned more than $34,39 an hour (or $71,540 annually).

Most workers in this field receive a benefits package that includes life and health insurance, paid vacation and sick leave, and a retirement pension.

Salary rates can vary depending on experience, geographic location, industry, and union membership. Approximately 54 percent of millwrights are represented by labor unions, one of the highest rates of membership for one profession. The International Union, United Automobile, Aerospace, and Agricultural Implement Workers of America; the International Association of Machinists and Aerospace Workers; and the United Brotherhood of Carpenters and Joiners of America are three unions to which millwrights belong.

WORK ENVIRONMENT

Approximately 40 percent of all millwrights work more than 40 hours a week. They often work overtime and in varying shifts to accommodate production schedules. Millwrights may be called to work at unusual times or for longer hours during emergencies. An equipment breakdown can affect an entire plant's operation and be very costly, so machines need to be immediately tended to when problems arise. Rearranging whole production lines often requires long hours.

Depending on the industry, working conditions vary from indoors to outdoors and from one location to much travel. In manufacturing jobs, millwrights work indoors in a shop setting. In construction jobs, they may work outside, in all weather conditions. Millwrights that do contract work may travel from plant to plant. Others are employed by a single manufacturer and remain on site much of the time.

What is consistent throughout the profession is the amount of labor involved. Millwrights often endure hard physical labor in surroundings made unpleasant by heat, noise, grime, and cramped spaces. In addition, the work can be hazardous at times, although protective gear and other safety regulations serve to protect workers from injury.

OUTLOOK

Employment for millwrights is expected to grow more slowly than the average for all occupations through 2014, according to the U.S. Department of Labor. New automation, the introduction of new, labor-saving technologies, limited growth in industrial construction, and the use of lower-paid workers for installation and maintenance of machinery are contributing to this slow growth.

However, millwrights will still be needed to keep existing machinery in working order, dismantle outdated machinery, and install new equipment. Many openings will arise each year as experienced workers transfer to other jobs or retire.

FOR MORE INFORMATION

For information about training and education programs, as well as legislative issues affecting the construction industry, contact
Associated General Contractors of America
2300 Wilson Boulevard, Suite 400
Arlington, VA 22201-3308
Tel: 703-548-3118
Email: info@agc.org
http://agc.org

For information on union membership, contact
International Association of Machinists and Aerospace Workers
9000 Machinists Place
Upper Marlboro, MD 20772-2687
Tel: 301-967-4500
http://www.goiam.org

International Union, United Automobile, Aerospace, and Agricultural Implement Workers of America
Solidarity House
8000 East Jefferson Avenue
Detroit, MI 48214-2699
Tel: 313-926-5000
http://www.uaw.org

For information on available publications, conventions and seminars, contact
National Tooling & Machining Association
9300 Livingston Road
Fort Washington, MD 20744-4914
Tel: 800-248-6862
http://www.ntma.org

To learn about apprenticeships and training programs and the benefits of union membership, visit the following Web site:
United Brotherhood of Carpenters and Joiners of America
50 F Street NW
Washington, DC 20001-1530
Tel: 202-546-6206
http://www.carpenters.org

Numerical Control Tool Programmers

OVERVIEW

Numerical control tool programmers, also called *computer numerical control tool programmers*, develop programs that enable machine tools to produce parts automatically. These precisely made parts are used in automobiles, airplanes, industrial machinery, and other durable goods. There are approximately 143,000 numerical control programmers and operators in the United States.

HISTORY

One of the earliest attempts to automate machinery occurred in the early 1700s, when a system of punched cards was used to control knitting machines in England. Holes in punched cards controlled mechanical linkages, which directed yarn colors and allowed various patterns to be woven into a piece of material. Automated machinery did not progress much further, though, until the computer was developed in the late 1940s.

The first use of numerical control (NC) was in 1947. John Parsons, owner of a helicopter rotor blade manufacturing company, experimented with regulating milling machinery through numerical control. He discovered that parts made through automated control were more accurate than those made manually. The U.S. Air Force, which had a need for uniquely shaped machined parts, contracted with Parsons and the Massachusetts Institute of Technology to develop a machine tool that could be programmed to make contoured parts automatically.

In 1952, they built the first numerically controlled machine tool. Shortly afterward, Giddings and Lewis, a large machine tool builder, built an NC profiling mill.

By 1958, other companies followed with NC machine tools of their own. Early NC tools used paper tapes to program machines. Machine commands were standardized and assigned numerical codes. These codes were then sequenced in the order in which the machine was to perform various operations. After these codes were punched onto a paper tape, a machine operator loaded the tape into a tape reader, loaded raw material, and started the machine. The machine ran automatically. As numerical control technology evolved, plastic tapes replaced paper, and magnetic spots rather than holes were used to represent codes. Unfortunately, this form of numerical control did not handle changes well; a whole new tape had to be created when process modifications were required. This was a slow and tedious process.

By the 1980s, computer numerical control (CNC) began to replace older NC methods. CNC programmers write computer programs to sequence the various steps a machine needs to complete. Many machines now have computers or microprocessors built into them. Programmers can easily revise the sequence of operations or other elements. In addition, these programs can store information about the machine tool operation (such as number and dimensions of parts made), request additional raw materials, and record maintenance requirements.

Another advancement in numerical control is direct numerical control, a process in which several machines are controlled by a central computer. This eliminates the need for individual machine control units and gives programmers more flexibility for modification and control.

The use of CNC machine tools has grown steadily during the last decade and is expected to increase in the future. New applications, such as versatile machining centers, are being developed that allow machines to provide multiple capabilities. Engineers and researchers continue to explore ways to improve the speed, precision, and versatility of machine processes through the use of numerical control and other automated processes.

THE JOB

Numerical control tool programmers write the programs that direct machine tools to perform functions automatically. Programmers must understand how the various machine tools operate and know the working properties of the metals and plastics that are used in the process.

Writing a program for a numerically controlled tool involves several steps. Before tool programmers can begin writing a program, they must analyze the blueprints of whatever function is to be performed or item to be made. Programmers then determine the steps and tools needed. After all necessary computations have been made, the programmers write the program.

Programmers almost always use computers to write the programs, using computer-aided design (CAD) systems. The growing use of this technology has increased productivity, translating designs directly into machine instructions without the need for coded programming. CAD systems allow programmers to more easily modify existing programs for other jobs with similar specifications.

To ensure that a program has been properly designed, tool programmers often perform a test or trial run. Trial runs help ensure that a machine is functioning properly and that the resulting product is according to plan. However, because problems found during a trial run could damage expensive machinery and tools, tests are increasingly done using computer simulations.

REQUIREMENTS

High School

High school courses in computer science, algebra, geometry, and English provide the basics needed to become a CNC programmer. More specific courses in blueprint reading, drafting, and computer-aided design are also useful. In addition, shop classes in metalworking can provide an understanding of machinery operations.

Postsecondary Training

Employers prefer to hire skilled machinists or tool operators to work as CNC programmers. Workers are usually trained through formal apprenticeships or postsecondary programs, or informally on the job. Apprenticeship programs usually last four years and include training in machine operations, program writing, computer-aided design and manufacturing, and analysis of drawings and design data. Classes include blueprint reading and drawing, machine tools, industrial mathematics, computers, and operation and maintenance of CNC machines.

Formal apprentice programs are becoming rare as more programmers receive training through community or technical colleges. Associate's degrees are available in areas such as manufacturing technology and automated manufacturing systems. Typical classes include machine shop, numerical control fundamentals, technical mechanics, advanced NC programming, introduction to robotic technology, and computer-assisted manufacturing.

For specialized types of programming, such as in aerospace or shipbuilding, employers often require a four-year degree in engineering in addition to technical skills and work experience.

Other Requirements

Numerical control tool programmers must have an understanding of machine tool operations, possess analytical skills, and show a strong aptitude for mathematics and computers. They also need good written and verbal communication skills to instruct machine operators and other engineers how to use and adjust programs. In addition, as new developments in technology bring new computer languages, methods, and equipment, numerical control tool programmers must be willing to learn new skills. Employers generally arrange and pay for courses to keep their programmers up-to-date on the latest trends and technology.

EXPLORING

If you are interested in a career as a tool programmer, you can test your interest and aptitude by taking shop and other vocational classes. You can also visit firms that employ numerical control tool programmers and talk directly with them to gain practical information about their jobs. Summer or part-time work at manufacturing firms and machine shops is a great way to find out more about the job and gain hands-on experience.

EMPLOYERS

Most numerical control tool programmers work in cities where factories and machine shops are concentrated, such as those located in the Northeast, Midwest, and West Coast regions. They work for many types and sizes of businesses. Among the largest employers are the aerospace and automobile industries and other manufacturers of durable goods. Approximately 143,000 numerical-control programmers and operators are employed in the United States.

STARTING OUT

Tool programming generally is not considered an entry-level job; most employers prefer to hire skilled machinists or those with technical training. Students who want to enter the job directly from formal training at a college or technical school can find job assistance through their school's career services office. Prospective programmers also may learn of openings through state and private employment offices, newspaper ads, and the Internet.

ADVANCEMENT

Advancement opportunities are somewhat limited for tool programmers. Employees may advance to higher-paying jobs by transferring to larger or more established manufacturing firms or shops. Experienced tool programmers who demonstrate good interpersonal skills and managerial ability can be promoted to supervisory positions.

EARNINGS

The median hourly salary for numeric control tool programmers was $20.42 (or $42,480 annually) in 2006, according to the U.S. Department of Labor. The lowest paid 10 percent earned less than $13.11 (or $27,260 annually), and the highest paid 10 percent earned more than $31.85 (or $66,260 annually).

Benefits vary but may include paid vacations and holidays, personal leaves, medical, dental, vision, and life insurance, retirement plans, profit sharing, and tuition assistance programs.

WORK ENVIRONMENT

Numerical control tool programmers generally work a 40-hour week, although overtime is common during peak periods. To justify the costly investments in machinery, some employers extend hours of operation, requiring CNC programmers to work evening and weekend shifts.

Programmers work in comfortable office surroundings, set apart from the noisier, more hazardous shop floor. Their work is more analytical and, as a result, less physically demanding than the work of machinists and other tool operators.

OUTLOOK

The employment of numerical control tool programmers is expected to decline through 2014, according to the *Occupational Outlook Handbook*. Initially, employment of CNC programmers was made possible by the introduction of new automation, but recent technological advancements are reducing the demand for such workers. Newer, user-friendly technology now allows some programming and minor adjustments to be made on the shop floor by machinists and machine operators rather than by skilled CNC programmers. Fewer programmers are needed to translate designs into CNC machine tool instructions, as new software is able to do this automatically. Employment is also influenced by economic cycles. As the demand for machined goods falls, programmers involved in this production may be laid off or forced to work fewer hours.

However, employers continue to have difficulty finding workers with the necessary skills and experience to fill open programmer positions. Additionally, many openings will arise as numerical control tool programmers leave jobs to retire or switch occupations.

FOR MORE INFORMATION

For information on apprenticeships, contact the UAW.

International Union, United Automobile, Aerospace, and Agricultural Implement Workers of America (UAW)
8000 East Jefferson Avenue
Detroit, MI 48214-2699
Tel: 313-926-5000
http://www.uaw.org

For information on careers and educational programs, contact the following organizations:

National Tooling & Machining Association
9300 Livingston Road
Fort Washington, MD 20744-4914
Tel: 800-248-6862
http://www.ntma.org

Precision Machined Products Association
6700 West Snowville Road
Brecksville, OH 44141-3212
Tel: 440-526-0300
http://www.pmpa.org

Packaging Engineers

OVERVIEW

Packaging engineers design, develop, and specify containers for all types of goods, such as food, clothing, medicine, housewares, toys, electronics, appliances, and computers. In creating these containers, some of the packaging engineer's activities include product and cost analysis, management of packaging personnel, development and operation of packaging filling lines, and negotiations with customers or sales representatives.

Packaging engineers may also select, design, and develop the machinery used for packaging operations. They may either modify existing machinery or design new machinery to be used for packaging operations.

HISTORY

Certain packages, particularly glass containers, have been used for about 4,500 years; the metal can was developed to provide food for Napoleon's army. However, the growth of the packaging industry developed during the industrial revolution, when shipping and storage containers were needed for the increased numbers of goods produced. As the shipping distance from producer to consumer grew, more care had to be given to packaging so goods would not be damaged in transit. Also, storage and safety factors became important with the longer shelf life required for goods produced.

Modern packaging methods have developed since the 1920s, with the introduction of cellophane wrappings. Since World War II, early packaging materials such as cloth and wood have been largely replaced by less expensive and more durable materials such as steel,

QUICK FACTS

School Subjects
Mathematics
Physics

Personal Skills
Mechanical/manipulative
Technical/scientific

Work Environment
Primarily indoors
Primarily one location

Minimum Education Level
Bachelor's degree

Salary Range
$45,822 to $70,200 to
$104,000

Certification or Licensing
Recommended (certification)
Required by certain states
(licensing)

Outlook
About as fast as the average

DOT
019

GOE
02.07.04

NOC
2148

O*NET-SOC
N/A

aluminum, and plastics such as polystyrene. Modern production methods have also allowed for the low-cost, mass production of traditional materials such as glass and paperboard. Government agencies, manufacturers, and designers are constantly trying to improve packaging so that it is more convenient, safe, and informative.

Today, packaging engineers must also consider environmental factors when designing packaging because the disposal of used packages has presented a serious problem for many communities. The United States uses more than 500 billion packages yearly; 50 percent of these are used for food and beverages and another 40 percent for other consumer goods. To help solve this problem, packaging engineers attempt to come up with solutions such as the use of recyclable, biodegradable, or less bulky packaging.

THE JOB

Packaging engineers plan, design, develop, and produce containers for all types of products. When developing a package, they must first determine the purpose of the packaging and the needs of the end users and their clients. Packaging for a product may be needed for a variety of reasons: for shipping, storage, display, or protection. A package for display must be attractive as well as durable and easy to store; labeling and perishability are important considerations, especially for food, medicine, and cosmetics. If the packaging purpose is for storage and shipping, then ease of handling and durability have to be considered. Safety factors are involved if the materials to be packaged are hazardous, such as toxic chemicals or explosives. Finally, the costs of producing and implementing the packaging have to be considered, as well as the packaging material's impact on the environment.

After determining the purpose of the packaging, the engineers study the physical properties and handling requirements of the product in order to develop the best kind of packaging. They study drawings and descriptions of the product or the actual product itself to learn about its size, shape, weight, and color, the materials used, and the way it functions. They decide what kind of packaging material to use and with the help of designers and production workers, they make sketches, draw up plans, and make samples of the package. These samples, along with lists of materials and cost estimates, are submitted to management or directly to the customer. Computer design programs and other related software may be used in the packaging design and manufacturing process.

When finalizing plans for packaging a product, packaging engineers contribute additional expertise in other areas. They are concerned with efficient use of raw materials and production facilities as well as conservation of energy and reduction of costs. For instance, they may use materials that can be recycled, or they may try to cut down on weight and size. They must keep up with the latest developments in packaging methods and materials and often recommend innovative ways to package products. Once all the details for packaging are worked out, packaging engineers may be involved in supervising the filling and packing operations, operating production lines, or drawing up contracts with customers or sales representatives. They should be knowledgeable about production and manufacturing processes, as well as sales and customer service.

After a packaging sample is approved, packaging engineers may supervise the testing of the package. This may involve simulation of all the various conditions a packaged good may be subjected to, such as temperature, handling, and shipping.

This can be a complex operation involving several steps. For instance, perishable items such as food and beverages have to be packaged to avoid spoilage. Electronic components have to be packaged to prevent damage to parts. Whether the items to be packaged are food, chemicals, medicine, electronics, or factory parts, considerable knowledge of the properties of these products is often necessary to make suitable packaging.

Design and marketing factors also need to be considered when creating the actual package that will be seen by the consumer. Packaging engineers work with graphic designers and packaging designers to design effective packaging that will appeal to consumers. For this task, knowledge of marketing, design, and advertising are essential. Packaging designers consider color, shape, and convenience as well as labeling and other informative features when designing packages for display. Very often, the consumer is able to evaluate a product only from its package.

The many different kinds of packages require different kinds of machinery and skills. For example, the beverage industry produces billions of cans, bottles, and cardboard containers. Often, packaging engineers are involved in selecting and designing packaging machinery along with other engineers and production personnel. Packaging can be manufactured either at the same facility where the goods are produced or at facilities that specialize in producing packaging materials.

The packaging engineer must also consider safety, health, and legal factors when designing and producing packaging. Various guidelines apply to the packaging process of certain products and the packaging engineer must be aware of these regulations. Labeling and packaging of products are regulated by various federal

Packaging Engineering Programs in the United States

Only a small number of colleges and universities in the United States offer programs in packaging science. Here is a list of some of the top programs. Visit their Web sites to learn more about typical classes, internships, and certificate and degree options.

Christian Brothers University (Memphis, Tenn.)
Tel: 877-321-4CBU
http://www.cbu.edu/engineering/packaging
Degrees available: Certificate

Clemson University (Clemson, S.C.)
Tel: 864-656-3390
http://www.clemson.edu/packaging
Degrees available: Bachelor's degree, master's degree

University of Florida (Gainesville)
Tel: 352-392-1864
http://www.agen.ufl.edu
Degrees available: Bachelor's degree

Indiana State University (Terre Haute)
Tel: 812-237-3353
http://www.indstate.edu/imt/acad_BS_PT.htm
Degrees available: Bachelor's degree

Michigan State University (East Lansing)
Tel: 517-353-4384
http://packaging.msu.edu
Degrees available: Bachelor's degree, master's degree, doctorate degree

Rochester Institute of Technology (Rochester, N.Y.)
Tel: 585-475-2411
http://www.rit.edu/~703www
Degrees available: Bachelor's degree, master's degree

University of Wisconsin-Stout (Menomonie)
Tel: 715-232-1246
http://www.uwstout.edu/programs/bsp
Degrees available: Bachelor's degree

agencies such as the Federal Trade Commission and the Food and Drug Administration. For example, the Consumer Product Safety Commission requires that safe packaging materials be used for food and cosmetics.

REQUIREMENTS

High School

During high school, take classes that will prepare you for a college engineering education. Concentrate on mathematics, including algebra, geometry, trigonometry, and calculus, as well as sciences, including physics and chemistry. You will also benefit from taking computer science, mechanical drawing, economics, and accounting classes. English, art, computer-aided design, and graphic arts classes are also recommended.

Postsecondary Training

Several colleges and universities offer a major in packaging engineering. These programs may be offered through an engineering school or a school of packaging within a university. Both bachelor of science and master of science degrees are available. It generally takes four or five years to earn a bachelor's degree and two additional years to earn a master's degree. A master's degree is not required to be a packaging engineer, although many professionals pursue advanced degrees, particularly if they plan to specialize in a specific area or do research. Many students take their first job in packaging once they have earned a bachelor's degree, while other students earn a master's degree immediately upon completing their undergraduate studies.

Students interested in this field often structure their own programs. In college, if no major is offered in packaging engineering, students can choose a related discipline, such as mechanical, industrial, electrical, chemical, materials, or systems engineering. It is useful to take courses in graphic design, computer science, marketing, and management.

Students enrolled in a packaging engineering program usually take the following courses during their first two years: algebra, trigonometry, calculus, chemistry, physics, accounting, economics, finance, and communications. During the remaining years, classes focus on core packaging subjects, such as packaging materials, package development, packaging line machinery, and product protection and distribution. Elective classes include topics concentrating on packaging and the environment, packaging laws and regulation, and technical classes on specific materials. Graduate studies, or those classes necessary to earn a master's degree, include advanced classes in design, analysis, and materials and packaging processes.

Certification or Licensing

The Institute of Packaging Professionals, a professional society, offers two levels of certification: certified professional in training (CPIT) and certified packaging professional (CPP). The CPIT is available to college students, recent graduates, and professionals who have less than six years of experience in the field. Requirements for this certification include passing a multiple-choice test and an essay test. The CPP can be earned by those with at least six years of experience in the field. In addition to the experience requirement, candidates must fulfill two other qualifications from the following: present a resume of activities, write a professional paper or hold a patent, pass a multiple-choice test, and pass an essay test. Although certification is not required, many professional engineers obtain it to show that they have mastered specified requirements and have reached a certain level of expertise.

For those interested in working within the specialized field of military packaging technology, the School of Military Packaging Technology offers a program resulting in certification as a military packaging professional. This program is cosponsored by the National Institute of Packaging, Handling, and Logistics Engineers. Generally, a person earns a bachelor of science degree in packaging engineering before taking these specialized courses.

Special licensing is required for engineers whose work affects the safety of the public. Much of the work of packaging engineers, however, does not require a license even though their work affects such factors as food and drug spoilage, protection from hazardous materials, and protection from damage. Licensing laws vary from state to state, but, in general, states have similar requirements. They require that an engineer must be a graduate of an approved engineering school, have four years of engineering experience, and pass the state licensing examination. A state board of engineering examiners administers the licensing and registration of engineers.

Other Requirements

Packaging engineers should have the ability to solve problems and think analytically and creatively. They must work well with people, both as a leader and as a team player. They should also be able to write and speak well in order to deal effectively with other workers and customers, and in order to document procedures and policies.

In addition, a packaging engineer should have the ability to manage projects and people.

EXPLORING

To get firsthand experience in the packaging industry, you can call local manufacturers to see how they handle and package their products. Often, factories will allow visitors to tour their manufacturing and packaging facilities.

Another way to learn about packaging is by observing the packaging that you encounter every day, such as containers for food, beverages, cosmetics, and household goods. Visit stores to see how products are packaged, stored, or displayed. Notice the shape and labeling on the container, its ease of use, durability for storage, convenience of opening and closing, disposability, and attractiveness.

You may also explore your aptitude and interest in a packaging career through graphic design courses, art classes that include construction activities, and computer-aided design classes. Participating in hobbies that include designing and constructing objects from different types of materials can also be beneficial. You can also learn about the industry by reading trade publications or visiting their Web sites, such as *Packaging World* (http://www. packworld.com) and *Packaging Digest* (http://www.packaging digest.com).

EMPLOYERS

Packaging engineers are employed by almost every manufacturing industry. Pharmaceutical, beverage, cosmetics, and food industries are major employers of packaging engineers. Some packaging engineers are hired to design and develop packaging while others oversee the actual production of the packages. Some companies have their own packaging facilities while other companies subcontract the packaging to specialized packing firms. Manufacturing and packaging companies can be large, multinational enterprises that manufacture, package, and distribute numerous products, or they can be small operations that are limited to the production of one or two specific products. Specialized packaging companies hire employees for all aspects of the packaging design and production process. Worldwide manufacturing offers career opportunities around the world. The federal government and the armed services also have employment opportunities for packaging engineers.

STARTING OUT

College graduates with a degree in packaging or a related field of engineering should find it easy to get jobs as the packaging industry continues its rapid growth. Many companies send recruiters to college campuses to meet with graduating students and interview them for positions with their companies. Students can also learn about employment possibilities through their schools' career services offices, job fairs, classified advertisements in newspapers and trade publications, and referrals from teachers. Students who have participated in an internship or work-study program through a college may learn about employment opportunities through contacts with industry professionals.

Students can also research companies they are interested in working for and apply directly to the person in charge of packaging or the personnel office.

ADVANCEMENT

Beginning packaging engineers generally do routine work under the supervision of experienced engineers and may also receive some formal training through their company. As they gain experience, they are given more difficult tasks and more independence in solving problems, developing designs, or making decisions.

Some companies provide structured programs in which packaging engineers advance through a sequence of positions to more advanced packaging engineering positions. For example, an entry-level engineer might start out by producing engineering layouts to assist product designers, advance to the position of product designer, and ultimately move into a management position.

Packaging engineers may advance from being a member of a team to a project supervisor or department manager. Qualified packaging engineers may advance through their department to become a manager or vice president of their company. To advance to a management position, the packaging engineer must demonstrate good technical and production skills and managerial ability. After years of experience, a packaging engineer might wish to become self-employed as a packaging consultant.

To improve chances for advancement, the packaging engineer may wish to get a master's degree in another branch of engineering or in business administration. Many executives in government and industry began their careers as engineers. Some engineers become patent attorneys by combining a law degree with their technical and scientific knowledge.

Many companies encourage continuing education throughout one's career and provide training opportunities in the form of in-house seminars and outside workshops. Taking advantage of any training offered helps one to develop new skills and learn technical information that can increase chances for advancement. Many companies also encourage their employees to participate in professional association activities. Membership and involvement in professional associations are valuable ways to stay current on new trends within the industry, to familiarize oneself with what other companies are doing, and to make contacts with other professionals in the industry. Many times, professionals learn about opportunities for advancement in new areas or at different companies through the contacts they have made at association events.

EARNINGS

Salaries for packaging engineers vary based on factors such as the industry in which they work (food and beverage, pharmaceuticals, cosmetics, personal care, etc.), the size of the employer, the area of the country in which they live, and their years of professional experience. A survey by Salary.com found the average entry-level salary for a packaging engineer in 2007 was $45,822 per year. The middle 50 percent of packaging engineers earned between $49,355 and $57,477, with senior-level packaging engineers easily earning more than $84,056 as they gain experience and advance within a company.

A survey conducted by Packworld.com found that the annual median salary, including bonus, of engineers was $70,200 in 2005. The average respondent reported earning $75,259. Corporate managers earned the highest average compensation, including salary and bonus, of $104,000.

Benefits vary from company to company but can include any of the following: medical, dental, and life insurance; paid vacations, holidays, and sick days; profit sharing; 401(k) plans; bonus and retirement plans; and educational assistance programs. Some employers pay fees and expenses for participation in professional associations.

WORK ENVIRONMENT

The working conditions for packaging engineers vary with the employer and with the tasks of the engineer. Those who work for companies that make packaging materials or who direct packaging operations might work around noisy machinery. Generally, they have offices near the packaging operations where they consult with others in their department, such as packaging machinery technicians and other engineers.

Packaging engineers also work with nontechnical staff such as designers, artists, and marketing and financial people. Packaging engineers must be alert to keeping up with new trends in marketing and technological developments.

Most packaging engineers have a five-day, 40-hour workweek, although overtime is not unusual. In some companies, particularly during research and design stages, product development, and the start up of new methods or equipment, packaging engineers may work 10-hour days or longer and work on weekends.

Some travel may be required, especially if the packaging engineer is also involved in sales. Also, travel between plants may be necessary to coordinate packaging operations. At various stages of developing packaging, the packaging engineer will probably be engaged in hands-on activities. These activities involve handling objects, working with machinery, carrying light loads, and using a variety of tools, machines, and instruments.

The work of packaging engineers also involves other, social concerns such as consumer protection, environmental pollution, and conservation of natural resources. Packaging engineers are constantly searching for safer, tamper-proof packaging, especially because harmful substances have been found in some food, cosmetics, and drugs. They also experiment with new packaging materials and utilize techniques to conserve resources and reduce the disposal problem. Many environmentalists are concerned with managing the waste from discarded packages. Efforts are being made to stop littering; to recycle bottles, cans, and other containers; and to use more biodegradable substances in packaging materials. The qualified packaging engineer, then, will have a broad awareness of social issues.

OUTLOOK

The packaging industry, which employs more than a million people, offers almost unlimited opportunities for packaging engineers. Packaging engineers work in almost any industry because virtually all manufactured products need one or more kinds of packaging. Some of the industries with the fastest growing packaging needs are food, drugs, and cosmetics.

The demand for packaging engineers is expected to be strong as newer, faster ways of packaging are continually being sought to meet the needs of economic growth, world trade expansion, and the environment. Increased efforts are also being made to develop packaging that is easy to open for the growing elderly population and those persons with disabilities.

FOR MORE INFORMATION

For information on certification, contact
Institute of Packaging Professionals
1601 North Bond Street, Suite 101
Naperville, IL 60563-0114
Tel: 630-544-5050
Email: info@iopp.org
http://www.iopp.org

For information on schools with packaging curriculum, contact
National Institute of Packaging, Handling, & Logistics Engineers
177 Fairsom Court
Lewisburg, PA 17837-6844
Tel: 866-464-7453
Email: niphle@dejazzd.com
http://www.niphle.org

For industry information, contact
Packaging Machinery Manufacturers Institute
4350 North Fairfax Drive, Suite 600
Arlington, VA 22203-1632
Tel: 888-275-7664
Email: pmmiwebhelp@pmmi.org
http://www.pmmi.org

For information on certification as a military packaging profes-
sional, contact
School of Military Packaging Technology
360 Lanyard Road
Aberdeen Proving Ground, MD 21005-5282
Tel: 410-278-4970
http://smpt.apg.army.mil

INTERVIEW

Dr. Scott Morris is an associate professor of food science and agricultural engineering at the University of Illinois at Urbana-Champaign. The university offers an internationally renowned packaging research and teaching program that is an adjunct to the school's degree programs in agricultural engineering and in food science and human nutrition. (Visit http://www.packaging.uiuc.edu to learn more about the program.) Dr. Morris discussed packaging science with the editors of Careers in Focus: Manufacturing.

Q. What types of students pursue packaging science study in your program?

A. Our students are typically those enrolled in programs that will lead to jobs in the food processing and packaging industry (including food science, chemical engineering, agricultural engineering, mechanical engineering, and industrial engineering). They are typically students who are looking for something a little different from the mainstream jobs that are usually offered to graduates of these programs.

Q. What advice would you offer packaging science majors as they graduate and look for jobs?

A. Maintain your personal networks, conduct your own job search, and do not depend on university job placement centers as your sole source of employment contacts.

Q. Are there any changes in this job market that students should expect? Have certain areas of this field been especially promising (or on the decline) in recent years?

A. The packaging industry, like many manufacturing industries, is increasingly moving offshore, so the types of jobs that are available may be either with end user companies (food or consumer products manufacturers), or involved in managing the packaging operations of offshore manufacturing assets. Basic operations such as film and bag manufacturing are on the decline in the United States, though I feel that many consumer packaging operations, such as final product packaging in the food or cosmetics industry, will remain domestic in the short term.

Pharmaceutical Production Workers

OVERVIEW

Pharmaceutical production workers manufacture and distribute pharmaceutical products. *Pharmaceutical operators* work with machines that perform such functions as filling capsules and inspecting the quality and weight of tablets. *Pharmaceutical supervisors and managers* oversee research and development, production, and sales and promotion workers. There are approximately 291,000 workers employed in the pharmaceutical industry in the United States.

HISTORY

The oldest known written records relating to pharmaceutical preparations come from the ancient Sumerians about 5,000 years ago. Other ancient cultures, such as the Indians and Chinese, used primitive pharmaceutical applications to eradicate evil spirits, which they believed to cause evil in the body. The Babylonians, Assyrians, Greeks, and Egyptians also compounded early pharmaceuticals in hope that they would rid the body of disease (which they believed was caused primarily by sinful thoughts and deeds).

Professions in pharmacy began to be established in the 17th century, after the first major list of drugs and their applications and preparations was compiled. The discoveries of the anesthetics morphine (first used in 1806), ether (1842), and cocaine (1860) were among the first pharmaceutical advancements to significantly benefit humankind. Since then, numerous vaccines have cured sickness and disease and have helped people live longer, healthier lives.

QUICK FACTS

School Subjects
Mathematics
Technical/shop

Personal Skills
Following instructions
Mechanical/manipulative

Work Environment
Primarily indoors
Primarily one location

Minimum Education Level
High school diploma

Salary Range
$24,565 to $46,332 to $56,160+

Certification or Licensing
None available

Outlook
Faster than the average

DOT
559

GOE
08.01.01, 08.03.02, 08.07.01

NOC
9232

O*NET-SOC
51-1011.00, 51-9011.00, 51-9199.99, 53-7064.00

Pharmaceutical production workers must be physically fit, mentally alert, and have the temperament to work at sometimes repetitive tasks. *(David Frazier, The Image Works)*

In 1852, the American Pharmaceutical Association (APA) was formed to help those in the pharmaceutical field organize their professional, political, and economic goals (the Pharmaceutical Manufacturers Association replaced the APA in 1958). Government intervention in the pharmaceutical industry began in 1848, and in 1931, the Food and Drug Administration was formed to provide legal regulation and monitoring of the pharmaceutical industry. As the industry became increasingly regulated and organized, qualified workers were sought to professionally produce and package pharmaceutical products. These workers, known collectively as pharmaceutical production workers, possess a variety of skills, responsibilities, and education levels and continue to actively work to improve the quality and length of our lives.

THE JOB

Pharmaceutical products are manufactured by production workers called, as a whole, pharmaceutical operators. Many of these employees work on production lines, tending equipment that measures, weighs, mixes, and granulates various chemical ingredients and components, which are then manufactured into such forms as pills and capsules. Often, these employees inspect the finished goods, looking for such inconsistencies as broken tablets and unfilled capsules.

There are a number of specific job designations in the realm of production.

Capsule filling machine operators run machines that fill gelatin capsules with medicine. They scoop empty capsules into a loading hopper and medicine into a filling hopper. After the filled and sealed capsules are ejected by the machinery, these operators inspect the capsules for proper filling and for evidence of breakage. They may also spot-check individual capsules or lots by comparing their weight with standardized figures on a weight specification sheet. This process is used for certain antihistamines, vitamins, and general pain relievers, for example.

Ampule and vial fillers work with glass tubes and plastic and glass containers with rubber stopules that are filled with medicine and then sealed. The process for filling is similar to that for the capsule filler; however, the operator must adjust gas flames to the appropriate temperature so that the tubes are completely sealed. They also count and pack readied ampules and vials for shipment. (Vials and syringes have recently become the primary containers for liquid drug production in the United States.)

Ampule and vial inspectors use magnifying glasses to check for cracks, leaks, and other damage. They keep records of inspected cartons, as well as damaged or flawed products.

Granulator machine operators operate mixing and milling machines that are equipped with fine blades that mix ingredients and then crush or mill them into powdered form so that they can be formed into tablets. They are responsible for weighing and measuring each batch, blending the ingredients with the use of machinery, and adding alcohol, gelatins, or starch pastes to help the pill keep its form. They then spread the mixture on trays that they place into an oven or steam dryer set at a predetermined temperature. At the conclusion of the heating process, they check each batch for dryness levels, size, weight, and texture.

Coaters operate machines that cover pills and tablets with coatings that flavor, color, or preserve the contents.

Fermenter operators oversee fermenting tanks and equipment, which produce antibiotics and other drugs. Operators start the mixing tanks, add ingredients, such as salt, yeast, and sugar, and transfer the mixture to a fermenting tank when it is ready. They are responsible for monitoring the temperature in the tanks, for adding precise amounts of liquid antibiotic, water, and foam-preventive oil, and for measuring the amount of solution so that it may be transferred to another tank for additional processing.

There are also a vast number of laborer professions involved in the production area of the pharmaceutical industry. *Hand packers and packagers* remove filled cartons from conveyor belts and transport other finished pharmaceutical products to and from shipping departments. *Industrial machinery mechanics* ensure that all machinery is working properly and at optimum production capacity.

Production managers direct workers in the manufacturing field by scheduling projects and deadlines. These employees also oversee factory operations and enforce safety and health regulations, monitor efficiency, and plan work assignments. They also direct and schedule assignments for the shipping department, which packs and loads the pharmaceutical products for distribution.

REQUIREMENTS

High School
If you're interested in a job as a production worker, take courses in math and science. You should also take courses, such as vo-tech, that will give you some background in machine work and engineering.

Postsecondary Education
Most employers offering production jobs require at least a high school diploma or the equivalent. Certain labor positions also require technical or vocational training.

Some pharmaceutical companies offer on-the-job training to nonprofessional workers. Various types of pharmaceutical training are also available in the military. Information about pharmaceutical careers in the armed forces can be obtained by contacting your nearest military recruitment office.

Other Requirements
Pharmaceutical production workers must be alert, dependable, and possess good communication skills, both oral and written. As workers interact with all divisions and levels of employees, strong communication skills promote faster and more accurate production. Production workers must also be physically fit, mentally alert to oversee production lines and processes, and have the temperament to work at sometimes repetitive tasks. Administrative and managerial workers must be decisive leaders with empathy for workers at all levels of education and responsibility.

EXPLORING

If your high school has a vocational training program, look into taking a class that prepares you for production work; a local community college may also have such a course. You should consider contacting

New Medicines in Development by Illness/Disease

1. Cancer: 682
2. Neurological disorders: 531
3. Infections: 341
4. Cardiovascular disorders: 303
5. Psychiatric disorders: 190
6. HIV/AIDS: 95
7. Arthritis: 88
8. Diabetes: 62
9. Alzheimer's disease and dementia: 55
10. Asthma: 60

Source: Pharmaceutical Research and Manufacturers of America, *Pharmaceutical Industry Profile 2006*

trade organizations such as the American Foundation for Pharmaceutical Education, whose objective is to improve pharmaceutical education programs and student performance. In addition, science-related clubs and social organizations often schedule meetings and professional lectures and offer career guidance as well.

EMPLOYERS

Production workers work for pharmaceutical companies that manufacture prescription and over-the-counter products. These companies include Johnson & Johnson, Merck, and Bristol-Myers Squibb. A small percentage of industry workers are employed with companies that make the biological products that are used by manufacturers in the production of drugs. Approximately 291,000 workers are employed in the pharmaceutical industry in the United States.

STARTING OUT

College-trained applicants often benefit from career services provided by the student services division of their schools. Applicants can also apply directly to pharmaceutical companies or through school contacts with professional organizations. In addition, newspapers and professional trade publications list job opportunities that are offered in each division and level of the industry.

ADVANCEMENT

There are many advancement opportunities for pharmaceutical workers. Production workers may advance to managerial positions and learn how to operate more sophisticated machinery. Administrators may become supervisors, executives, sales managers, or marketing executives.

There are always possibilities for advancement for employees who are willing to develop new skills and take on more responsibilities. Many positions, however, require additional, formal training.

EARNINGS

Because the pharmaceutical industry is a large field, earnings vary tremendously and depend on the worker's position, educational background, and amount of work experience. However, some generalizations can be made about certain wages.

According to the *Career Guide to Industries*, which is published by the U.S. Department of Labor, production workers in drug manufacturing averaged approximately $891 per week (or $46,332 annually) in 2006. The wage range for these employees is broad, depending on the size of the firm, the shift to which the worker is assigned, years at the company, and the geographic location of the plant. Overtime compensation is usually equal to time and a half or double time. The *Career Guide to Industries* also reports the following median hourly earnings for pharmaceutical industry workers in 2006: supervisors/managers of production and operating workers, $27.00 ($56,160 annually); chemical equipment operators and tenders, $17.10 ($35,568 annually); inspectors, testers, sorters, samplers, and weighers, $15.69 ($32,635 annually); mixing and blending machine setters, operators, and tenders, $14.22 ($29,578 annually); and packaging and filling machine operators and tenders, $11.81 ($24,565 annually).

All full-time workers, regardless of their work specialty, receive paid vacations, medical and dental insurance, paid sick and personal days, pension plans, and life insurance. Some workers may also be offered profit-sharing, savings plans, and reimbursement for job-related education.

WORK ENVIRONMENT

Production workers average 45-hour workweeks and eight hours per shift; at some pharmaceutical firms, however, shifts may run round-the-clock, meaning that some employees work a variety of shifts. Production workers often work in chemicals factories, which are well ventilated and offer good lighting but may be noisy and crowded. These workers may have to package products and load them onto trucks or docks by hand or with forklifts. Machinery operators may stand during much of their shift. Laborers and packagers frequently walk, stand, bend, and lift in the course of their day. They may be required to operate machinery to lift heavy or bulky material. Ampule and vial fillers wear special clothing, such as complete face and body coverings, to maintain sterile conditions. Safety equipment is required for hazardous tasks of all types.

Managers work in office environments that are often modern, neat, and have good lighting and ample workspaces. They often bring work home with them or have late meetings with other staff members.

OUTLOOK

As the number of people age 65 and over continues to increase, the pharmaceutical industry is expected to grow to accommodate medical needs. In addition, technological developments continue to be pursued in many scientific endeavors, including the creation of new drugs for the treatment of such widespread diseases as AIDS and cancer. The overall employment outlook for workers in the pharmaceutical industry is thus considered very good and is anticipated to continue growing at a strong pace through 2014, according to the U.S. Department of Labor.

Many pharmaceutical manufacturing companies are investigating growth in health-related areas, such as cosmetics, veterinary products, agricultural chemicals, and medicinals and botanicals—which may create additional employment opportunities for pharmaceutical production workers.

FOR MORE INFORMATION

For more information about the pharmaceutical industry, contact the following organizations:

American Foundation for Pharmaceutical Education
One Church Street, Suite 202
Rockville, MD 20850-4184
Tel: 301-738-2160
Email: info@afpenet.org
http://www.afpenet.org

Pharmaceutical Research and Manufacturers of America
950 F Street, NW
Washington, DC 20004-1438
Tel: 202-835-3400
http://www.phrma.org

Plastics Products Manufacturing Workers

OVERVIEW

Plastics products manufacturing workers mold, cast, and assemble products made of plastics materials. The objects they make include dishes, signs, toys, insulation, appliance parts, automobile parts, combs, gears, bearings, and many others.

HISTORY

Thermoplastics—plastics that soften with heat and harden when cooled—were invented in France in 1828. In the United States in 1869, a printer named John Wesley Hyatt attempted to create an alternative material to supplement ivory in billiard balls. He experimented with a mixture of cellulose nitrate and camphor, creating what he called celluloid. His invention, patented in 1872, brought about a revolution in production and manufacturing. By 1892, over 2,500 articles were being produced from celluloid. Among these inventions were piano keys, false teeth, and the first movie film. Celluloid did have its drawbacks. It could not be molded and it was highly flammable.

It was not until 1909, however, that the Belgian-American chemist Leo H. Baekeland produced the first synthetic plastic. This product replaced natural rubber in electrical insulation and was used for phone handsets and automobile distributor caps and rotors. It is still used today. Other plastics materials have been developed steadily. The

QUICK FACTS

School Subjects
Mathematics
Technical/shop

Personal Skills
Following instructions
Mechanical/manipulative

Work Environment
Primarily indoors
Primarily one location

Minimum Education Level
High school diploma

Salary Range
$16,640 to $25,563 to
$42,058+

Certification or Licensing
Voluntary

Outlook
More slowly than the
average

DOT
553

GOE
08.02.01

NOC
9214

O*NET-SOC
51-4011.00, 51-4021.00,
51-4022.00, 51-4023.00,
51-4031.00, 51-4032.00,
51-4033.00, 51-4034.00,
51-4035.00, 51-4061.00,
51-4062.00, 51-4072.00,
51-4081.00, 51-4191.00,
51-4192.00, 51-4193.00

greatest variety of materials and applications, however, came during World War II, when the war effort brought about a need for innovation in clothing, consumer goods, transportation, and military equipment.

Today, plastics manufacturing is a major industry whose products play a vital role in many other industries and activities around the world. It is difficult to find an area of our lives where plastics do not play some role. Major users of plastics include the electronics, packaging, aerospace, medical, and housing and building industries. The plastics industry also provides the makings for a large variety of consumer goods. Appliances, toys, dinnerware, luggage, and furniture are just a few products that require plastics.

Plastics products manufacturing workers have always been needed in the production of plastic. Their job responsibilities and skills have changed and grown more specialized as new production processes and materials have come into widespread use.

THE JOB

Plastics are usually made by a process called polymerization, in which many molecules of the same kind are combined to make networks of giant particles. All plastics can be formed or shaped; some become pliable under heat, some at elevated room temperatures. When treated, some plastics become hard, some incredibly strong, and some soft like putty.

Plastic objects are formed using several different methods. Each method produces a different type of plastic. In compression molding, plastics compounds are compressed and treated inside a mold to form them. In injection molding, liquid plastic is injected into a mold and hardened. Blow molding is like glass blowing—air is forced into plastic to make it expand to the inner surface of a mold. In extrusion, hot plastic is continuously forced through a die to make products like tubing. Laminating involves fusing together resin-soaked sheets, while the calender process forms sheets by forcing hot plastic between rollers. Finally, in fabrication, workers make items out of solid plastic pieces by heating, sawing, and drilling.

Marvin Griggs works for a company called Centro, in Springdale, Arkansas. "We're a rotational molder for plastic products," Griggs says. "We make custom parts for companies like John Deere. We don't produce our own product. They send the mold, we build the parts." Griggs is part of a four-person crew running one of the machines. The machine operator and assistant operator pour resin into the molds, which is then placed into the oven, and then the cooler. They open the molds and remove and inspect the part for warping or some other defect. The trimmer then trims the line, cutting off the plastic flange. "If the part needs holes cut into it, or fixtures put in it," Griggs says, "they pass it down to me." The tools he uses include pneumatic hand tools, routers, and a large tank. "The parts are dunk-tested to make sure they're sealed, and there are no holes. We have a tight quality control system."

While plastics compounds may be mixed in plastics-materials plants, plastics manufacturers sometimes employ blenders, or color mixers, and their helpers to measure, heat, and mix materials to produce or color plastic materials. *Grinding-machine operators* run machines that grind particles of plastics into smaller pieces for processing. *Pilling-machine operators* take plastics powder and compress it into pellets or biscuits for further processing. Other workers (*plastic form makers* and *plastics patternmakers*) are responsible for making the molds and patterns that are used to determine the shape of the finished plastics items. *Foam-machine operators* spray thermoplastic resins into conveyor belts to form plastic foam.

Many plastics products plants make goods according to clients' specifications. When this is the case, *job setters*, using their knowledge of plastics and their properties, adjust molding machines to clients' instructions. They make such adjustments as changing the die through which the plastic flows, adjusting the speed of the flow, and replacing worn cutting tools when necessary. Then the machine is ready to accept the plastic and produce the object.

Injection molders operate machines that liquefy plastic powders or pellets, inject liquid plastic into a mold, and eject a molded product. Compact discs, toys, typewriter keys, and many other common products are made by injection molding. Injection workers set and observe gauges to determine the temperature of the plastic and examine ejected objects for defects.

One common plastic is polystyrene, which when molded using heat and pressure makes cast foam products such as balls, coolers, and packing nests. *Polystyrene-bead molders* operate machines that expand these beads and mold them into sheets of bead board. *Polystyrene-molding-machine tenders* run machines that mold pre-expanded beads into objects. At the end of the molding cycle, they lift the cast objects from the molds and press a button to start the machine again.

Extruder operators and their helpers set up and run machines that extrude thermoplastics to form tubes, rods, and film. They adjust the dies and machine screws through which the hot plastic is drawn, adjust the machine's cooling system, weigh and mix plastics materials, empty them into the machine, set the temperature and speed of the machine, and start it.

Blow-molding-machine operators run machines that mold objects such as bleach bottles and milk bottles by puffing air into plastic to expand it. *Compression-molding-machine operators* run machines that mold thermosetting plastics into hard plastic objects. Thermosetting plastics are those that harden because of a chemical reaction rather than by heating and cooling.

Casters make similar molded products by hand. *Strippers* remove molded items from molds and clean the molds. Some molded products must be vacuum cured and *baggers* run machines that perform this task.

Plastic sheeting is formed by *calender operators*, who adjust the temperature, speed, and roller position of machines that draw plastic between rollers to produce sheets of specified thickness. *Stretch-machine operators* stretch plastic sheets to specified dimensions. *Preform laminators* press fiberglass and resin-coated fabrics over plaster, steel, or wooden forms to make plastic parts for boats, cars, and airplanes.

Other common plastics products are fiberglass poles and dowels. *Fiberglass-dowel-drawing-machine operators* mount dies on machines, mix and pour plastics compounds, draw fiberglass through the die, and soak, cool, cure, and cut dowels. *Fiberglass tube molders* make tubing used in fishing rods and golf club shafts.

Plastics that are not molded may be cut into shapes. *Shaping-machine operators* cut spheres, cones, blocks, and other shapes from plastic foam blocks. *Pad cutters* slice foam rubber blocks to specified thicknesses for such objects as seat cushions and ironing board pads.

Many products undergo further processing to finish them. *Foam-gun operators* reinforce and insulate plastic products such as bathtubs and auto body parts by spraying them with plastic foam. *Plastic-sheet cutters* use power shears to cut sheets, following patterns glued to the sheets by pattern hands. *Sawyers* cut rods, tubes, and sheets to specified dimensions. *Trimmers* trim plastic parts to size using a template and power saw. *Machine finishers* smooth and polish the surface of plastic sheets. And *plastics heat welders* use hot-air guns to fuse together plastic sheets.

Hand finishers trim and smooth products using hand tools and sandpaper. *Buffers* remove ridges and rough edges from fiberglass or plastic castings. *Sponge buffers* machine-buff the edges of plastic sponges to round them, and *pointing-machine operators* round the

Facts about the U.S. Plastics Industry, 2005

- Approximately 1.1 million people were employed in the plastics industry.
- Annual shipments from the plastics industry amounted to approximately $341 billion—making it the fourth largest manufacturing industry.
- There were 18,246 plastics manufacturing and wholesale trade establishments throughout the United States.
- The top 10 states for plastics industry employment were: California, Ohio, Texas, Michigan, Illinois, Indiana, Pennsylvania, New York, Wisconsin, and North Carolina.

Source: Society of the Plastics Industry

points on the teeth of plastic combs. *Edge grinders* tend machines that square and smooth edges of plastic floor tile.

Assemblers and *laminated plastics assemblers and gluers* assemble pieces to form certain products. These may include skylights and wet suits. Plastics inspectors inspect and test finished products for strength, size, uniformity, and conformity to specifications.

Experienced workers supervise plastics-making departments, and the industry also employs unskilled workers such as *laborers* to help haul, clean, and assemble plastics materials, equipment, and products.

REQUIREMENTS

High School

If you are interested in the plastics products manufacturing field, take courses in mathematics, chemistry, physics, computer science, shop, drafting, and mechanical drawing. English and speech classes will help build good communication and interpersonal skills.

Postsecondary Training

Most employers of plastics products manufacturing workers require applicants have a high school diploma. You will learn most of your skills on the job. In extrusion plants, trainees can become Class I extruders after about three months. Other jobs require training from one to 12 months.

Applicants with some knowledge of chemistry, mathematics, physics, drafting, industrial technology, or computer science have a better chance of being hired. Some colleges offer associate's or bachelor's degrees in plastics technology. Job seekers with these degrees have a definite competitive edge and may also advance more quickly.

Another training option is to participate in an apprenticeship program. Apprenticeships provide experience and a chance to explore the field. Apprenticeships in tool and die making for plastics last four or five years and teach through classroom instruction and on-the-job training. A high school education is normally a prerequisite for an apprenticeship.

Certification or Licensing

Certification is not required of plastics technicians, but the National Certification in Plastics program is available through the Society of the Plastics Industry (SPI). As industry equipment becomes more complex, employers may prefer to hire only certified technicians. To become a certified operator, you will take an exam in one of four areas: blow molding, extrusion, injection molding, or thermoforming. The exam is geared toward skilled employees such as machine operators, process technicians, setup technicians, and supervisors.

Other Requirements

You must have mechanical aptitude and manual dexterity to work well with tools and various materials. Lifting equipment and materials takes some strength, and workers who operate machines stand much of the time. You must be able to work well with others and follow oral and written directions, and you must be precise and organized in your work.

"I'm really particular about my work from being in construction for six years," Marvin Griggs says. "I pay really close attention to detail."

EXPLORING

Many high schools are beginning to offer vocational programs, and other apprenticeship opportunities, for those interested in becoming technicians; some of these programs have courses geared specifically toward preparation for the plastics industry. SPI is currently involved in providing career direction to young people interested in the plastics industry. Contact SPI (http://www.plasticsindustry.org) for career and industry information. You can also learn about the industry by reading trade magazines such as *Modern Plastics* (http://www.modplas. com) or *Plastics News* (http://www.plasticsnews.com).

EMPLOYERS

Major plastics employers in the United States include DuPont, General Motors, and Owens Corning. Some of the top thermoforming companies are in Illinois: Pactiv Corporation, Solo Cup Company, and Ivex Packaging LLC are a few of them. Michigan has some of the top injection molding companies, including Lear Corporation and Venture Industries Corporation, but large plastics companies are located all across the country.

STARTING OUT

After receiving your high school diploma, you should apply directly to the personnel departments of plastics plants in the area in which you wish to work. Newspaper ads may list openings in the industry, and state employment agencies may also provide leads. The Web site http://www.polysort.com features a virtual job fair that offers free access to job listings in the plastics industry.

ADVANCEMENT

In the plastics industry, advancement comes with experience, skill, and education. Because plants like to teach workers their own methods, and because skilled plastics workers are scarce, most plastics companies promote workers from within to fill more responsible and higher paying jobs. Plastics workers who understand machine setup and the properties of plastics advance more quickly than those limited to machine operations.

Workers who pursue associate's or bachelor's degrees in plastics technology have the best chances for advancement. With advanced training and experience, some plastics workers may become plastics engineers or mold designers. Others may move into supervisory, management, or sales and marketing positions. Apprenticeships, such as in tool and die manufacturing, may also lead to more highly paid production work.

EARNINGS

According to the U.S. Department of Labor, earnings for material handlers in the plastics industry vary widely, depending on the job. Median earnings in 2006 ranged from of $12.29 per hour (about $25,563 annually) or less for molding, coremaking, and casting machine setters, tenders, and operators, to $20.22 per hour (about $42,058 annually) or more for model makers. Entry-level jobs may pay as low as $8 per hour or $16,640 per year.

In addition to salary, many employers offer medical and dental benefits, life insurance, paid sick leave, personal and vacation days, and retirement plans. Employees may also be able to participate in profit-sharing plans.

WORK ENVIRONMENT

Most plastics industry workers work 40 hours per week. Because plants operate on three shifts, entry-level workers may work nights and move to day shifts as they gain experience and seniority.

Plastics plants are generally safe, well lighted and ventilated, and modern. Workers must observe safety precautions when working around hot machines and plastics, sharp machine parts, and electrical wiring, and when sawing, cutting, or drilling plastics parts. Plastics work, however, is not usually strenuous. Workers use machines to lift heavy dies and other equipment.

As with most production work, jobs in the plastics industry often demand a fair amount of repetition. Workers who need great variety in their jobs may not enjoy production work. Plastics plants tend to be smaller than many other types of factories so a sense of teamwork often develops among the production workers. Such camaraderie can lead to increased job satisfaction and enjoyment.

"There are some safety issues," Marvin Griggs says, "working with power tools." But he hasn't encountered too many negatives since taking the job, despite the many hours on his feet and being restricted to certain areas most of the day. He benefits from a retirement plan and profit sharing and has an employer who makes an effort to get to know the members of the company.

OUTLOOK

Increased competition in foreign markets and the introduction of laborsaving technology will reduce opportunities for plastics products manufacturing workers. As a result, the U.S. Department of Labor predicts that employment for workers in this field will grow more slowly than the average for all occupations through 2014—although employment outlooks vary by occupation. Multiple machine tool operators and plastics-molding, core-making, and casting machine operators should enjoy good job prospects in the next several years. Occupations that may experience a decline in employment include grinding-machine operators (due to automation); blenders; cutting, punching, and press machine setters, operators, and tenders; and color mixers.

FOR MORE INFORMATION

The Plastics Division of the American Chemistry Council offers a great deal of information about the plastics industry and maintains an informative Web site.

Plastics Division of the American Chemistry Council
1300 Wilson Boulevard
Arlington VA 22209-2323
Tel: 703-741-5000
http://www.plastics.org

For information about scholarships, seminars, and training, contact
Plastics Institute of America
UMass-Lowell Campus, Wannalancit Center
600 Suffolk Street
CVIP, 2nd Floor South
Lowell, MA 01854-3643
Tel: 978-934-3130
Email: contactus@plasticsinstitute.org
http://www.plasticsinstitute.org

For information on careers, college programs, and certification, contact
Society of the Plastics Industry
1667 K Street, NW, Suite 1000
Washington, DC 20006-1605
Tel: 202-974-5200
http://www.socplas.org

For information about certification, visit the following Web site provided by the Society of the Plastics Industry:
National Certification in Plastics
http://www.certifyme.org

Quality Control Engineers and Technicians

OVERVIEW

Quality control engineers plan and direct procedures and activities that will ensure the quality of materials and goods. They select the best techniques for a specific process or method, determine the level of quality needed, and take the necessary action to maintain or improve quality performance. *Quality control technicians* assist quality control engineers in devising quality control procedures and methods, implement quality control techniques, test and inspect products during different phases of production, and compile and evaluate statistical data to monitor quality levels.

HISTORY

Quality control technology is an outgrowth of the industrial revolution, which began in England in the 18th century. Each person involved in the manufacturing process was responsible for a particular part of the process. The worker's responsibility was further specialized by the introduction of manufacturing with interchangeable parts in the late 18th and early 19th centuries. In a manufacturing process using this technique, a worker concentrated on making just one component, while other workers concentrated on creating other components. Such specialization led to increased production efficiency, especially as manufacturing processes became mechanized during the early part of the 20th century. It also meant, however, that no one worker was responsible for the overall quality of the product. This led to the need for another kind of specialized production worker whose primary responsibility was not one aspect of the product but rather its overall quality.

This responsibility initially belonged to the mechanical engineers and technicians who developed the manufacturing systems, equipment, and procedures. After World War II, however, a new field emerged that was dedicated solely to quality control. Along with specially trained persons to test and inspect products coming off assembly lines, new instruments, equipment, and techniques were developed to measure and monitor specified standards.

At first, quality control engineers and technicians were primarily responsible for random checks of products to ensure they met all specifications. This usually entailed testing and inspecting either finished products or products at various stages of production.

During the 1980s, a renewed emphasis on quality spread across the United States. Faced with increased global competition, especially from Japanese manufacturers, many U.S. companies sought to improve quality and productivity. Quality improvement concepts such as Total Quality Management, Six Sigma, continuous improvement, quality circles, and zero defects gained popularity and changed the way in which companies viewed quality and quality control practices. A new philosophy emerged, emphasizing quality as the concern of all individuals involved in producing goods and directing that quality be monitored at all stages of manufacturing, not just at the end of production or at random stages of manufacturing.

Today, most companies focus on improving quality during all stages of production, with an emphasis on preventing defects rather than merely identifying defective parts. There is an increased use of sophisticated automated equipment that can test and inspect products as they are manufactured. Automated equipment includes cameras, X rays, lasers, scanners, metal detectors, video inspection systems, electronic sensors, and machine vision systems that can detect the slightest flaw or variance from accepted tolerances. Many companies use statistical process control to record levels of quality and determine the best manufacturing and quality procedures. Quality control engineers and technicians work with employees from all departments of a company to train them in the best quality methods and to seek improvements to manufacturing processes to further improve quality levels.

Many companies today are seeking to conform to international standards for quality, such as ISO 9000 and ISO 14000, in order

A technician checks the quality of pasta on a production line. *(Corbis)*

to compete with foreign companies and to sell products to companies and individuals around the world. These standards are based
on concepts of quality of industrial goods and services and involve
documenting quality methods and procedures.

THE JOB

Quality control engineers are responsible for developing, implementing, and directing processes and practices that result in a desired
level of quality for manufactured parts. They identify standards to
measure the quality of a part or product, analyze factors that affect
quality, and determine the best practices to ensure quality.

Quality control engineers set up procedures to monitor and control quality, devise methods to improve quality, and analyze quality
control methods for effectiveness, productivity, and cost factors.
They are involved in all aspects of quality during a product's life
cycle. Not only do they focus on ensuring quality during production
operations, they are also involved in product design and evaluation. Quality control engineers may be specialists who work with
engineers and industrial designers during the design phase of a
product, or they may work with sales and marketing professionals to evaluate reports from consumers on how well a product is

performing. Quality control engineers are responsible for ensuring that all incoming materials used in a finished product meet required standards and that all instruments and automated equipment used to test and monitor parts during production perform properly. They supervise and direct workers involved in assuring quality, including quality control technicians, inspectors, and related production personnel.

Quality control technicians work with quality control engineers in designing, implementing, and maintaining quality systems. They test and inspect materials and products during all phases of production in order to ensure that they meet specified levels of quality. They may test random samples of products or monitor production workers and automated equipment that inspect products during manufacturing. Using engineering blueprints, drawings, and specifications, they measure and inspect parts for dimensions, performance, and mechanical, electrical, and chemical properties. They establish tolerances, or acceptable deviations from engineering specifications, and they direct manufacturing personnel in identifying rejects and items that need to be reworked. They monitor production processes to ensure that machinery and equipment are working properly and are set to established specifications.

Quality control technicians also record and evaluate test data. Using statistical quality control procedures, technicians prepare charts and write summaries about how well a product conforms to existing standards. Most importantly, they offer suggestions to quality control engineers on how to modify existing quality standards and manufacturing procedures. This helps to achieve the optimum product quality from existing or proposed new equipment.

Quality control technicians may specialize in any of the following areas: product design, incoming materials, process control, product evaluation, inventory control, product reliability, research and development, and administrative applications. Nearly all industries employ quality control technicians.

REQUIREMENTS
High School
To prepare for this career, take high school classes in mathematics (including algebra, geometry, and statistics), physical sciences, physics, and chemistry. You should also take shop, mechanical drawing, and computer courses. In addition, you should take English courses that develop your reading skills, your ability to write well-organized reports with a logical development of ideas, and your ability to speak comfortably and effectively in front of a group.

Postsecondary Training

Quality control engineers generally have a bachelor's degree in engineering. Many quality control engineers receive degrees in industrial or manufacturing engineering. Some receive degrees in metallurgical, mechanical, electrical, chemical engineering, or business administration, depending on where they plan to work. College engineering programs vary based on the type of engineering program. Most programs take four to five years to complete and include courses in mathematics, physics, and chemistry. Other useful courses include statistics, logistics, business management, and technical writing.

Educational requirements for quality control technicians vary by industry. Most employers of quality control technicians prefer to hire applicants who have received some specialized training. A small number of positions for technicians require a bachelor of arts or science degree. In most cases, though, completion of a two-year technical program is sufficient. Students enrolled in such a program at a community college or technical school take courses in the physical sciences, mathematics, materials control, materials testing, and engineering-related subjects.

Certification or Licensing

Although there are no licensing or certification requirements designed specifically for quality control engineers or technicians, some need to meet special requirements that apply only within the industry employing them. Many quality control engineers and technicians pursue voluntary certification from professional organizations to indicate that they have achieved a certain level of expertise. The American Society for Quality, for example, offers certification at a number of levels including quality engineer certification, quality process analyst, and quality technician certification. Requirements include having a certain amount of work experience, having proof of professionalism (such as being a licensed professional engineer), and passing a written examination. Many employers value this certification and take it into consideration when making new hires or giving promotions.

Other Requirements

Quality control engineers need scientific and mathematical aptitudes, strong interpersonal skills, and leadership abilities. Good judgment is also needed, as quality control engineers must weigh all the factors influencing quality and determine procedures that incorporate price, performance, and cost factors.

Quality control technicians should do well in mathematics, science, and other technical subjects and feel comfortable using the language and symbols of mathematics and science. Good eyesight and good manual skills, including the ability to use hand tools, are required, as is the ability to follow technical instructions and make sound judgments about technical matters. Quality control technicians should have orderly minds and be able to maintain records, conduct inventories, and estimate quantities.

EXPLORING

Quality control engineers and technicians work with scientific instruments; therefore, academic or industrial arts courses that introduce you to different kinds of scientific or technical equipment will be beneficial. You should also take electrical and machine shop courses, mechanical drawing courses, and chemistry courses with lab sections. Joining a radio, computer, or science club is also a good way to gain experience and to engage in team-building and problem-solving activities. Active participation in clubs is a good way to learn skills that will benefit you when working with other professionals in manufacturing and industrial settings. To find out more about engineering in general, join the Junior Engineering Technical Society (JETS), which will give you the opportunity to test your skills and meet professionals and others interested in engineering, math, and science. (Visit the JETS Web site at http://www.jets.org.)

Keep in mind that quality control activities and quality control professionals are often directly involved with manufacturing processes. If it is at all possible, try to get a part-time or summer job in a manufacturing setting, even if you are not specifically in the quality control area. Although the work may entail menial tasks, it will give you firsthand experience in the environment and demonstrate the depth of your interest to future employers.

EMPLOYERS

There are approximately 160,000 industrial production managers (a group that includes quality control engineers) and 69,000 industrial engineering technicians (a group that includes quality control technicians) working in the United States. The majority of quality control engineers and technicians are employed in the manufacturing sector of the economy. Because engineers and technicians work in all areas of industry, their employers vary widely in size, product, location, and prestige.

STARTING OUT

Students enrolled in two-year technical schools may learn of openings for quality control technicians through their schools' career services office. Recruiters often visit these schools and interview graduating students for technical positions. Quality control engineers also may learn of job openings through their schools' career services office, recruiters, and job fairs. In many cases, employers prefer to hire engineers who have some work experience in their particular industry. For this reason, applicants who have had summer or part-time employment or participated in a work-study or internship program have greater job opportunities.

Students may also learn about openings through help wanted ads or by using the services of state and private employment services. They may also apply directly to companies that employ quality control engineers and technicians. Students can identify and research such companies by using job resource guides and other reference materials available at most public libraries.

ADVANCEMENT

Quality control technicians usually begin their work under the direct and constant supervision of an experienced technician or engineer. As they gain experience or additional education, they are given assignments with greater responsibilities. They can also become quality control engineers with additional education. Promotion usually depends on additional training as well as job performance. Technicians who obtain additional training have greater chances for advancement opportunities.

Quality control engineers may have limited opportunities to advance within their companies. However, because quality control engineers work in all areas of industry, they have the opportunity to change jobs or companies to pursue more challenging or higher paying positions. Quality control engineers who work in companies with large staffs of quality personnel can become quality control directors or advance to operations management positions.

EARNINGS

Earnings vary according to the type of work, the industry, and the geographical location. Quality control engineers earn salaries comparable to other engineers. According to the U.S. Department of Labor, the median yearly income for industrial production managers was

$77,670 in 2006. The lowest paid 10 percent earned less than $47,230, and the highest paid 10 percent made more than $130,680.

The average annual salary for industrial engineering technicians was $46,810 in 2006, according to the U.S. Department of Labor. Salaries ranged from less than $30,190 to more than $79,180.

Most companies offer benefits that include paid vacations, paid holidays, and health insurance. Actual benefits depend on the company but may also include pension plans, profit sharing, 401(k) plans, and tuition assistance programs.

WORK ENVIRONMENT

Quality control engineers and technicians work in a variety of settings, and their conditions of work vary accordingly. Most work in manufacturing plants, though the type of industry determines the actual environment. For example, quality control engineers in the metals industry usually work in foundries or iron and steel plants; conditions there are hot, dirty, and noisy. Other factories, such as for the electronics or pharmaceutical industries, are generally quiet and clean. Most engineers and technicians have offices separate from the production floor, but they still need to spend a fair amount of time there. Engineers and technicians involved with testing and product analysis work in comfortable surroundings, such as a laboratory or workshop. Even in these settings, however, they may be exposed to unpleasant fumes and toxic chemicals. In general, quality control engineers and technicians work inside and are expected to do some light lifting and carrying (usually not more than 20 pounds). Because many manufacturing plants operate 24 hours a day, some quality control technicians may need to work second or third shifts.

As with most engineering and technical positions, the work can be both challenging and routine. Engineers and technicians can expect to find some tasks repetitious and tedious. In most cases, though, the work provides variety and satisfaction from using highly developed skills and technical expertise.

OUTLOOK

The employment outlook for quality control engineers and technicians depends, to some degree, on general economic conditions. The U.S. Department of Labor projects slower than average growth through 2014 for the field of industrial production management, which includes quality control engineers and technicians. This is a result of increased productivity as a result of better technology, in addition to a greater reliance on manufacturing workers to constantly monitor the quality of their own work. However, the roles of the quality control engineer and technicians are vital to production and cannot be eliminated. Thus, there will still be new jobs to replace people retiring from or otherwise leaving this field.

Many companies are making vigorous efforts to make their manufacturing processes more efficient, lower costs, and improve productivity and quality. Opportunities for quality control engineers and technicians should be good in the food and beverage industries, pharmaceutical firms, electronics companies, and chemical companies. Quality control engineers and technicians may find employment in industries using robotics equipment or in the aerospace, biomedical, bioengineering, environmental controls, and transportation industries. Lowered rates of manufacturing in the automotive and defense industries will decrease the number of quality control personnel needed for these areas. Declines in employment in some industries may occur because of the increased use of automated equipment that tests and inspects parts during production operations.

FOR MORE INFORMATION

For information on certification and student chapters, contact
American Society for Quality
PO Box 3005
Milwaukee, WI 53201-3005
Tel: 800-248-1946
Email: help@asq.org
http://www.asq.org

ASTM International offers seminars and other training programs for those involved in testing materials and quality assurance. Visit its Web site to read articles from its magazine Standardization News.
ASTM International
100 Barr Harbor Drive
PO Box C700
West Conshohocken, PA 19428-2959
Tel: 610-832-9585
http://www.astm.org

INTERVIEW

Rick Munoz has been a quality assurance laboratory technician at a dental equipment manufacturing company for more than three years. He discussed his career with the editors of Careers in Focus: Manufacturing.

Q. Why did you decide to enter this field?

A. I became a quality assurance lab tech to build a technical foundation in my career path.

Q. How did you train for this career? What was your educational path?

A. I received technician's training for this career. I earned a bachelor of science in electronics engineering technology.

Q. Take me through a day in your life as a quality assurance laboratory technician.

A. I arrive and check the progress of all current product/material tests and resume the respective procedures for each test. Tests vary in requirements including the longevity of materials being tested, product durability through accelerated life testing, corrosion resistance to typical product usage, and the consistency of performance of new products or prototypes. All tests are diligently recorded on an everyday basis under strict guidelines. Once the test results are recorded, I create a formal report for presentation to engineers, and in some high-profile product cases, management. Quite often, I'm asked to do a retest with a refined product to see if the modification engineers have made based on prior testing improves the test result; this cycle can last a few days, or with complex products, several weeks.

Sporting Goods Production Workers

OVERVIEW

Sporting goods production workers manufacture, assemble, and finish sporting goods equipment such as golf clubs, fishing tackle, basketballs, footballs, skis, and baseball equipment. Their tasks range from operating machines to fine handcrafting of equipment.

HISTORY

Throughout history, every society and culture has developed games and sports for relaxation and competition. Bowling, for example, has been around for centuries; a stone ball and nine stone pins were found in the ancient tomb of an Egyptian child. Polo is believed to have originated in Asia and was brought back to England and America by British officers returning from India in the 1800s. Native American peoples played lacrosse with webbed sticks and hard wooden balls centuries ago. Soccer, arguably the world's most popular sport, was invented in England, where a version of the game was played nearly 2,000 years ago.

Some of the most popular sports in America have a relatively recent history. Basketball was invented in 1891 by Dr. James Naismith in Springfield, Massachusetts; its popularity grew so quickly that it became an Olympic event in 1936. Ice hockey as we know it was invented in Canada in the 1870s. It quickly became popular in northern countries and was inaugurated as an Olympic sport in 1920. In the 1870s, football started as a college sport that mixed elements of soccer and rugby and soon developed its own set of rules. Although folklore attributes the invention of baseball to Abner Doubleday in 1839, people were playing it for many years before then.

Some games, both ancient and modern, have changed little since the time they were first played. Soccer, for instance, has remained popular in part because of its simplicity; the only equipment needed to play is a ball. Other sports have grown to require more elaborate equipment. Modern technology has been applied to many aspects of sport and given us such improvements as better protective padding, livelier tennis rackets, and stronger golf balls. Computers are used to improve the design and composition of sports gear. The equipment used in each sport is unique in design and manufacture and is put together by skilled specialists.

THE JOB

Every sport involves its own equipment, and each kind of equipment is made somewhat differently. Basketballs and volleyballs are made by approximately the same process, which differs from the processes for making footballs and baseballs. But the manufacturing processes for sporting goods and for other products are also similar in many ways.

As in the manufacturing of other products, *machine operators* control large machine tools, such as presses, and smaller tools, such as saws and sewing machines. After they have done their tasks, they may pass the work on to different kinds of assemblers. *Floor assemblers* operate large machines and power tools; *bench assemblers* work with smaller machines to complete a product and perhaps to test it; *precision assemblers* perform highly skilled assembly work. They may work closely with engineers and technicians to develop and test new products and designs. These general categories can be applied to many of the occupations involved in sporting goods manufacturing, although the job titles vary with different kinds of products.

In the manufacturing of golf equipment, for example, the shaft of a golf club and the head, or club end, are made separately and are then assembled, weighted, and balanced. *Golf-club assemblers* do much of the work. They use bench-mounted circular saws to cut the shaft for a club to a specified length, depending on the model of club being made. *Golf-club head formers* hammer precast metal club heads to the correct angle and then glue the proper club head onto a shaft and secure the head by drilling a small hole and inserting a pin. Wooden clubs are glued together the same way, except that once the assembly has dried, the weight of the club is checked and adjusted for the model type. *Assemblers* or *golf-club weighters* can adjust the weight by drilling a hole into the head and adding molten lead or threaded cylindrical metal weights.

Grip wrappers attach the handle of the golf club. They insert a club in a rotating machine, brush adhesive on the shaft, attach a leather strap, and then carefully spin the shaft to cover it tightly and evenly with the leather strap. When they are finished, they trim the excess leather and fasten the grip in place with tape or a sleeve. Finally, *golf-club head inspectors* examine the head to verify that it conforms to specifications.

The manufacturing of fishing equipment is another instance of a production process involving a series of workers. It begins with *fishing-rod markers,* who mark the places on rod blanks where the line guides and decorative markings should be put. After this, *fishing-rod assemblers* use liquid cement to attach the hardware, such as reel seats, handles, and line guides, onto the rods. Line guides can also be attached with thread by *guide winders,* who decorate the rods by winding thread around them at intervals. Finally, *fishing-reel assemblers* assemble the parts of the intricate reel mechanisms, test the reels, and then attach them to rods.

Some processes used in manufacturing sporting goods, such as lathing (which is used in making baseball bats) and vulcanizing (which is used in making hockey pucks), are commonly used in making many other products as well. But other processes are more specialized. To make basketballs, volleyballs, and soccer balls, for example, *ball assemblers* cement panels of rubberized fabric onto a hollow, spherical frame made of wax. A door opening is left in the ball carcass so that the wax frame can be broken and removed piece by piece. Once this is done, a bladder is inserted into the ball and inflated to a specific pressure. The flaps of the door opening are then aligned with the other seams of the ball and cemented onto the bladder, and the ball is complete.

Some baseball equipment is still made by hand, much the same way it was many years ago. Many wooden bats are hand-turned to the specifications of each player. Danny Luckett makes Louisville Slugger bats in Louisville, Kentucky, and has personally finished bats for many major league players. "We used to do everything by hand, but now a tracing machine helps make the bats," says Luckett, who has worked for 30 years for the Hillerich & Bradsby Company, which is the manufacturer of Louisville Slugger bats. "The machine is similar to a key-making machine and uses a template. Before, we could make 32 to 35 in a day, and now we can make 250 to 260 in a day."

Baseballs themselves are assembled by *hand baseball sewers,* who cement the leather hide of the ball to the core and sew the sections of hide together using a harness needle and waxed linen thread. To make baseball gloves, *lacers* sew precut pieces of leather together, working with the glove inside out. Then, *lining inserters* put a lining in place, and *reversers* turn the glove right-side out on a series of posts. Next, *baseball glove shapers* use a heated, hand-shaped form to open and stretch the finger linings. With various rubber mallets, they hammer the seams smooth and form the glove pocket. Finally, they try on the glove and pound the pocket to make sure that it fits comfortably.

As these examples show, the manufacturing of sporting goods involves ordinary industrial processes that are adapted to suit each product. Within the limits of sports safety and economical operation of their plants, sporting goods manufacturers are constantly trying to improve designs and manufacturing processes to make equipment that is reliable and durable and maximizes athletic performance.

REQUIREMENTS

While most employers prefer that employees have a high school diploma, it is not a requirement for many jobs in this industry.

The Most Popular Team Sports

The following is a list of the most popular team sports in the United States in 2006 and the corresponding number of participants (in millions) age six and above.

Basketball	32.0
Volleyball (court, grass, beach)	20.9
Football (touch, tackle)	18.2
Soccer	17.0
Softball (slow pitch, fast pitch)	15.1
Baseball	10.3
Cheerleading	4.2
Ice hockey	2.6
Lacrosse	1.6

Source: *Sports Participation Topline Report, 2006 Edition,* Sporting Goods Manufacturers Association

Employers look for workers who can do accurate, high-quality work at a fast pace. Most employees in the industry learn their skills through on-the-job training. Training may take from a few days to several months, depending on the job.

High School
High school courses that can help prepare students for working in the sporting goods equipment industry include shop, basic mathematics, blueprint reading, sewing, and other classes that provide practice in following written instructions and diagrams or making items by hand. Speech classes will also be helpful. "It's important to have good communication skills," says Danny Luckett. "You have to pay attention to details."

Postsecondary Training
Electronic devices are used more and more in sports for purposes such as timing skiers and runners. As more applications are developed for electronic and electrical equipment, more manufacturing workers will be needed who have the kind of knowledge and training that is available at technical schools. Also, design, precision assembly, and production jobs increasingly rely on machinery that is controlled by computers. For these reasons, a background that includes training in electronics and computer applications is very important for many jobs in this industry.

Other Requirements
Sports equipment production workers generally need good eyesight and manual dexterity to work with small parts and operate machines. Interest in sports can be an advantage. For example, it helps for workers who shape baseball gloves to have experience playing baseball and using gloves, so they know the feel of a good fit.

"I used to play [baseball] when I was younger," says Luckett. "It's kind of neat now to watch the games and know that we have a part in it."

Some sporting goods production workers belong to labor unions. Luckett belongs to the United Steelworkers of America. Another union is UNITE HERE, which represents workers who make shoes, caps, hats, uniforms, ski suits, golf gloves, leotards, and other apparel. Other unions include the United Food and Commercial Workers International Union; the International Textile, Garment and Leather Workers' Federation; the Laborers' International Union of North America; the International Brotherhood of Electrical Workers; and the International Brotherhood of Boilermakers, Iron Ship Builders, Blacksmiths, Forgers, and Helpers.

EXPLORING

To learn something about what the work is like in the sporting goods production business, try to get a summer job working in a nearby sports equipment factory. Such a job is likely to be in a warehouse or in custodial services, but it may still offer you a chance to observe the manufacturing processes firsthand and to talk with experienced employees about their jobs. Working part time can also be an opportunity to show an employer that you are dependable and have good work habits, and it could lead to permanent employment in the future. Since an interest in sports is helpful, a knowledge of sports and sports equipment gained through actual participation would be beneficial.

EMPLOYERS

There are more than 3,000 manufacturers of sporting goods equipment in the United States, according to the Sporting Goods Manufacturers Association (SGMA). They are located throughout the United States and may be small companies or large conglomerates. The recent trend toward mergers has affected this industry; fewer companies are employing more workers.

STARTING OUT

Job seekers in this field can contact sporting goods manufacturers directly to learn whether or not they have any job openings. Other possibilities for job leads include checking the listings at the local offices of the state employment service and in the classified sections of newspapers. School counselors can provide information about local companies that are looking for workers.

ADVANCEMENT

Newly hired employees in sporting goods factories usually are assigned simple tasks. Trainees may acquire their job skills informally as they work beside and watch more experienced workers. Others may enter into a formal training program. Workers who have completed training for their job category and have shown they can meet production requirements may be able to move into higher paying production jobs as they become available.

"Here, you're not really hired to do one specific job, but jobs are filled from within and you start where there is an opening," says Danny Luckett about the baseball bat manufacturer for which he works.

In companies that are large and diversified, workers may advance to jobs in other divisions. Qualified employees may also move to positions as product inspectors or supervisors of other production workers. Moving into management jobs usually requires further experience, technical training, and formal education in business subjects.

Some knowledgeable, experienced people with new product ideas or an urge for independence may decide to start their own sporting goods production company. Setting up a new business in any field is a risky venture, however, and anyone who is interested in taking this step needs first to take a hard and informed look at the high costs involved, in addition to the potential benefits.

EARNINGS

According to the U.S. Department of Labor, the median hourly earnings of machine setters, operators and tenders ranged from about $8 to $20 in 2006 (or $16,640 to $41,600 annually for full-time work). Assemblers had earnings than ranged from less than $8 an hour to $19 or more per hour in 2006. Beginning workers often start at between minimum wage and $8.50 per hour ($10,700 to $17,680 annually for full-time work). Wages are generally higher for skilled, experienced machine operators. Most workers also get fringe benefits, such as health insurance, paid holidays and vacation days, and pension plans. Some firms offer stock options to employees.

WORK ENVIRONMENT

Conditions in plants vary, with some factories having modern, well-equipped, well-lit work stations for employees. Other plants provide less comfortable working conditions. In some jobs, employees have to sit or stand in one place for the entire work shift, while other jobs require heavy lifting, hammering, or other physically strenuous activities. People who operate presses, molds, and other heavy machinery may have to load and remove heavy work pieces made of leather, metal, fiberglass, plastic, and other materials. Almost all workers have production quotas to meet, which can be stressful at times.

Heat, noise, dust, or strong odors are unavoidable in many production jobs. Workers may need to wear safety glasses, hard hats, earplugs, or other protective clothing.

Sports equipment production workers average 40 hours of work per week. Many factories operate two or three shifts a day, so employees may be required to work days, evenings, nights, or weekends.

OUTLOOK

As sports and fitness become more popular among health-conscious Americans, the market for sporting goods is expected to continue to grow. Exports of American-made goods may also increase in coming years.

This does not mean, however, that the number of jobs in sporting goods manufacturing will also increase. The manufacture of many kinds of sports gear is very labor-intensive, and to keep labor costs down, manufacturers have moved some of their operations to plants in other countries, where workers can be paid lower wages. In addition, advances in automation, robotics, and computer-aided manufacturing are allowing companies to phase out certain production jobs. In the future, the need will be for employees who can program machines, supervise production, and manage resources. Workers will also be needed to test product safety and quality.

The sporting goods manufacturing industry is generally a solid but not expanding business. Job turnover is fairly high among production and assembly workers, so most new workers will be hired to replace people who leave their jobs.

FOR MORE INFORMATION

For industry information and job listings, contact
Sporting Goods Manufacturers Association
1150 17th Street, NW
Washington, DC 20036-4603
Tel: 202-775-1762
Email: info@sgma.com
http://sgma.com

Toy Industry Workers

OVERVIEW

Toy industry workers create, design, manufacture, and market toys and games to adults and children. Their jobs are similar to those of their counterparts in other industries. Some work on large machines, while others assemble toys by hand. According to the U.S. Bureau of Labor Statistics, more than half of all employees in the toy industry work in production. Most toy companies are located in or near large metropolitan areas.

HISTORY

Recreational games have roots in ancient cultures. For example, backgammon, one of the oldest known board games, dates back about 5,000 years to areas around the Mediterranean. Chess developed in about the sixth century in India or China and was based on other ancient games.

Dolls and figurines also have turned up among old artifacts. Some seem to have been used as playthings, while others apparently had religious or symbolic importance. More recently, European kings and noblemen gave elaborate dolls in fancy costumes as gifts. Fashion styles thus were spread through other regions and countries. Doll makers in cities such as Paris, France, and Nuremberg, Germany, became famous for crafting especially beautiful dolls. Over the years dolls have been made of wood, clay, china, papier-mâché, wax, and hard rubber, and they have been collected and admired by adults as well as children.

For centuries, most toys were made by hand at home. Mass production began in the 19th century during the industrial revolution.

QUICK FACTS

School Subjects
Mathematics
Technical/shop

Personal Skills
Mechanical/manipulative
Technical/scientific

Work Environment
Primarily indoors
Primarily one location

Minimum Education Level
High school diploma

Salary Range
$17,000 to $35,000 to $150,000+

Certification or Licensing
None available

Outlook
About as fast as the average

DOT
731

GOE
08.03.06

NOC
9619

O*NET-SOC
N/A

In the 20th century, one of the most enduringly popular toys was the teddy bear, named after President Theodore Roosevelt.

Toy companies generally devise their own products or adapt them from perennial favorites, but they occasionally buy ideas for new toys and games from outsiders. One famous example of this was a board game devised during the Great Depression by an out-of-work man in his kitchen. He drew a playing board on his tablecloth using the names of streets in his hometown of Atlantic City and devised a game that let him act out his fantasies of being a real estate and business tycoon. The game, which he called Monopoly, became one of the most popular games of all time.

The popularity of certain toys rises and falls over time. Some toys maintain their popularity with successive generations of children or experience a comeback after a few years. Computer and video games have boomed during the past decade and will undoubtedly continue to become more complex and realistic as technology advances. Still, it is very difficult to predict which new toys will become popular. Introducing a new toy into the marketplace is a gamble, and that adds excitement and pressure to the industry.

THE JOB

Taking a toy from the idea stage to the store shelf is a long and complex operation, sometimes requiring a year or two or even longer. Ideas for new toys or games may come from a variety of sources. In large companies, the marketing department and the research and development department review the types of toys that are currently selling well and devise new toys to meet the perceived demand. Companies also get ideas from professional inventors, freelance designers, and other people, including children, who write to them describing new toys they would like to see made.

Toy companies consider ideas for production that they sometimes end up scrapping. A toy company has two main considerations in deciding whether to produce a toy: the degree of interest children (or adults) might have in playing with the toy and whether the company can manufacture it profitably.

A toy must be fun to play with, but there are measures of a toy's worth other than amusement. Some toys are designed to be educational, develop motor skills, excite imagination and curiosity about the world, or help children learn ways of expressing themselves.

Often manufacturers test new ideas to determine their appeal to children. *Model makers* create prototypes of new toys. *Marketing researchers* in the company coordinate sessions during which groups of children play with prototype toys. If the children in the test group enjoy a toy and return to play with it more than a few times, the toy has passed a major milestone.

The company also has to ask other important questions: Is the toy safe and durable? Is it similar to other toys on the market? Is there potential for a large number of buyers? Can the toy be mass-produced at a low enough cost per toy to ensure a profit? Such questions are usually the responsibility of *research and development workers,* who draw up detailed designs for new toys, determine materials to be used, and devise methods to manufacture the toy economically. After the research and development workers have completed their work, the project is passed on to engineers who start production.

Electronic toys, video games, and computer games have skyrocketed in popularity in the past decade. The people who develop them include *computer engineers, technicians,* and *software programmers. Technical development engineers* work on toys that involve advanced mechanical or acoustical technology. *Plastics engineers* work on plans for plastic toys. They design tools and molds for making plastic toy parts, and they determine the type of molding process and plastic that are best for the job. Plastics engineers who work for large firms may design and build 150 or more new molds each year.

To determine the best way to manufacture a toy, *manufacturing engineers* study the blueprints for the new product and identify necessary machinery. They may decide that the company can modify equipment it already has, or they may recommend purchasing new machinery. Throughout the engineering process, it is important to find ways to minimize production costs while still maintaining quality.

After selecting the equipment for production, *industrial engineers* design the operations of manufacturing: the layout of the plant, the time each step in the process should take, the number of workers needed, the ways to measure performance, and other detailed factors. Next, the engineers teach supervisors and assembly workers how to operate the machinery and assemble the new toy. They inform shift supervisors the rate of production the company expects. Industrial engineers might also be responsible for designing the process of packaging and shipping the completed toys.

As toys are being built on the assembly line, *quality control engineers* inspect them for safety and durability. Most toy companies adhere to the quality standards outlined in ASTM F963, a set of voluntary guidelines the toy industry has developed for itself. The toy industry is also monitored by the Consumer Products Safety Commission and must adhere to various federal laws and standards that cover the safety of toys under normal use and any foreseeable misuse or abuse.

Finally, getting the toys from the factory to the store shelf is the responsibility of *sales and merchandising workers*. These employees stay in contact with toy stores and retail outlets and arrange for toy displays and in-store product promotions.

Factory workers on assembly lines mass-produce practically all toys and games. The manufacturing processes can be as unique as the toys themselves. Workers first cast pieces of plastic toys in injection molds and then assemble them. They machine, assemble, and finish or paint wooden and metal toys. They make board games employing many of the same printing and binding processes used for books. They print the playing surface on a piece of paper, glue it to a piece of cardboard of the proper size, and tape the two halves of the board together with bookbinding equipment.

Toy assemblers put together various plastic, wood, metal, and fabric pieces to complete toys. They may sit at a conveyor belt or workbench, where they use small power tools or hand tools, such as pliers and hammers, to fasten the pieces together. Other toy assemblers operate larger machines such as drill presses, reamers, flanging presses, and punch presses. On toys such as wagons that are made on assembly lines, assemblers may do only a single task, such as attaching axles or tires. Other toys may be assembled entirely by one person; for instance, one person at one station on an assembly line may attach the heads, arms, and legs of action figures.

The manufacture of dolls provides a good example of the various manual and mechanical operations that can go into the making of a single toy. Plastic doll *mold fillers* make the head, torso, arms, and legs of the doll in plastic-injection molds. Other workers cure and trim the molded parts and send them off on a conveyor belt. The doll's head may go to a *rooter operator*, who operates a large machine that roots or stitches a specific quantity of synthetic hair onto the head. After attaching the hair in the form of a wig, a *doll wigs hackler* combs and softens synthetic hair by pulling it through a hackle, which is a combing tool with projecting bristles or teeth. Then, a *hair finisher* sets the hair in the specified style by combing, brushing, and cutting. A toy assembler puts together the doll's parts, and a *hand finisher* completes the doll by dressing it in clothes and shoes. An *inspector* examines the completed doll to make sure it meets the original specifications and then sends it on for packaging and shipment.

REQUIREMENTS

High School
Obtain your high school diploma before pursuing any job in the toy industry. Some positions, such as industrial engineer and software

programmer, also require that you complete postsecondary education. If one of these jobs interests you, be sure to take a college prep curriculum. If you are interested in production work, you will probably not need formal education beyond high school. While in high school, be sure to take shop classes that teach you how to use machinery. Family and consumer science classes in which you learn about sewing, using patterns, and selecting materials may also be helpful. Other classes to take include art, basic mathematics, and English.

Postsecondary Training

Because of the wide range of jobs in the toy industry, people with a variety of educational backgrounds are employed in the field. Those in supervisory, research, and design positions may hold bachelor's or graduate degrees in various fields, including art, electronics, engineering, architecture, psychology, business, and the sciences. Those working in production positions, such as rooter operators and toy assemblers, typically learn how to do their work during on-the-job training, which lasts anywhere from several days to a few weeks.

Other Requirements

Production workers need patience and the ability to do repetitive work. Good hand-eye coordination is required for those doing detailed tasks, such as painting designs on toys. The ability to be creative and to understand consumers' wants are especially important for toy designers. Those operating machinery, such as rooter operators, must be able to complete their work quickly and accurately. Many positions also require that the worker have a good sense of color. Many toy industry workers belong to the labor union International Union of Allied Novelty and Production Workers.

EXPLORING

One way to find out more about toys and the toy industry is to become familiar with the consumer, that is, children. If you have a younger brother or sister, observe what toys he or she plays with most and try to determine why. Think about what toys you enjoyed as a child and figure out what was appealing to you. Spend time at a neighborhood day care center or a children's hospital ward or babysit to learn more about what kids like to play with and why.

Read industry magazines to learn more about trends in the business. *Playthings* magazine, for example, is one such publication. It also has a Web site (http://www.playthings.com) featuring the latest industry news.

You can also get part-time or summer work at a toy store. This will give you the opportunity to see what new toys are on the market, how companies advertise and promote their toys, and what types of toys parents and children buy.

If there is a toy manufacturer in your area, apply for a summer or part-time job with the company. The most likely areas to find jobs are in assembly work, sales, and marketing. A large portion of toys sell in the period before Christmas, so toy companies must have their products ready ahead of time. The months from July through September are usually the busiest in the year, and jobs may be most available during this time.

EMPLOYERS

The most popular locations for toy companies in the United States are the largest cities and states, such as New York, Los Angeles, Chicago, and San Francisco, as well as Washington, Texas, Florida, New Jersey, Connecticut, and Pennsylvania.

In large toy firms, workers with many different titles may be involved in each of the activities described. Sometimes workers are grouped in teams, such as the research and development team. As a team, the members consider research and development aspects of every toy the company makes. In smaller firms, job distinctions may not be so precise and separate. A group of employees may work together on the entire process of developing and marketing a toy from the beginning to the end. The fewer employees in a firm, the more functions they can perform.

Some workers are employed on a temporary basis, manufacturing toys during the busiest season, which is before Christmas.

STARTING OUT

For entry-level positions in the toy industry, job seekers can contact the personnel offices of toy manufacturers. This is true for most toy factory jobs, whether applicants are looking for engineering, management, marketing, or factory production jobs. Some job listings and information may be available at the local offices of the state employment service, at local union offices, or in newspaper classified ads.

ADVANCEMENT

In general, advancement to better jobs and higher pay depends on acquiring skills, further education, and seniority. Some production workers advance by learning to operate more complex machinery. Reliable, experienced workers in production jobs might be promoted to supervisory positions. Professional and management staff can progress in various ways depending on their areas of expertise.

EARNINGS

Earnings in this field vary by the type of job a person does, the size of the employer, and the employer's location. Some production workers are paid on a piecework basis; that is, they are paid according to the number of pieces of work that they complete. Others are paid on a straight salary. Most production workers work 40-hour workweeks. Machine operators usually earn more than assemblers who work by hand. During the peak production season from July to September, factory workers may have to work long shifts, and they are paid overtime rates for the extra hours. Newly hired production workers may be paid at rates slightly above the federal minimum wage and have annual incomes of approximately $17,000. With experience, they may earn as much as $22,000 per year. According to the U.S. Department of Labor, inspectors, testers, and sorters (a classification including toy inspectors) earned median hourly wages of $14.14 in 2006. This wage translated to median yearly earnings of approximately $29,411, with a range in salary from a low of $17,992 to a high of $51,688. Most production workers are unionized, and wage scales and conditions for wage increases are often set according to agreements between the union and company management.

Management and engineers are often paid a straight salary. Salary ranges vary from company to company and especially from job to job. For example, research and development employees can start at about $25,000 per year; some may eventually work their way up to $150,000 or more annually. Salary levels for these workers depend on their job responsibilities, experience, seniority, and quality of work. According to the U.S. Department of Labor, commercial and industrial designers (including toy designers or model makers) had median yearly earnings of $54,560 in 2006. Those in the top 10 percent of the salary range earned more than $92,970. The bottom 10 percent of commercial and industrial designers earned less than $31,510. The department also reports the median annual income for industrial engineers as $68,620 in 2006. The highest paid 10 percent of industrial engineers earned more than $100,980, and the lowest paid 10 percent earned less than $44,790 during that same period.

In addition to wages, many workers receive other benefits, such as health and life insurance coverage, pension plans, and vacations.

WORK ENVIRONMENT

The production floor of some toy factories is simply a large room in which workers perform routine tasks. A factory may employ as many as several hundred people to do production work. Some people work at machines, while others sit at tables or assembly lines. Some workers stand throughout much of the day. Workers often have to meet production schedules and quotas, so they have to keep up a brisk work pace. Some people are bored by the repetition in many production jobs, because they must do the same few tasks over and over for long periods.

In smaller companies, the work may be highly seasonal. Getting the company's products ready for selling in the Christmas season, and to some extent, the Easter season, can mean that employees are asked to put in 10 or more hours of work a day. And if the company makes a product that becomes extremely popular, workers may have to scramble to make enough of the item to keep up with demand. But in the off-peak season, usually the winter months, and in average conditions, production workers may have reduced hours or may be laid off. In many shops, some production workers are employed only five or six months a year. Management and other professional employees work year-round. They may need to put in overtime hours during peak seasons or before trade shows, but they do not earn overtime pay.

OUTLOOK

According to the Toy Industry Association, industry sales of traditional toys totaled $21.3 billion in 2005, which was a slight decrease from the previous year. Although there is always a demand for toys, this industry is definitely affected by downward trends in the economy. Employment outlooks, however, depend on factors such as the type of job done, the amount of automation introduced into the workplace, and the amount of production that is moved overseas.

Overall, employment for production workers in the U.S. toy industry will probably remain steady or increase slightly as the economy improves. Sales of games and puzzles, arts and crafts, and learning and exploration toys have gone up in the past year, which may create more job opportunities for toy workers with skills or experience in these areas. Additionally, video games that are popular with older children and even adults should make the future bright for this segment of the industry. On the other hand, some video games or game parts are imports from abroad, which may limit the number of new jobs to be found here. Also, if toy preferences change, employment patterns may shift in coming years in ways that are hard to predict now. Nevertheless, there is a fairly high rate of job turnover among production workers due in part to the low pay and repetitive work. Because of this, replacement workers are usually needed.

For those in other areas of the industry, such as design, engineering, and marketing, employment outlooks should follow the overall health of the toy industry as well as the economy.

FOR MORE INFORMATION

For information on postsecondary programs in toy design, contact the following schools:

Fashion Institute of Technology
Seventh Avenue at 27th Street
New York, NY 10001-5992
Tel: 212-217-7999
Email: FITinfo@fitnyc.edu
http://www.fitnyc.edu

Otis College of Art and Design
Toy Design Program
9045 Lincoln Boulevard
Los Angeles, CA 90045-3505
Tel: 310-665-6985
Email: toydesign@otis.edu
http://www.otis.edu

To learn more about the toy industry, toy news, and the American International Toy Fair, contact

Toy Industry Association
1115 Broadway, Suite 400
New York, NY 10010-3450
Tel: 212-675-1141
Email: info@toy-tia.org
http://www.toy-tia.org

Index